D1710593

West's Law School
Advisory Board

JESSE H. CHOPER
Professor of Law,
University of California, Berkeley

DAVID P. CURRIE
Professor of Law, University of Chicago

YALE KAMISAR
Professor of Law, University of San Diego
Professor of Law, University of Michigan

MARY KAY KANE
Chancellor, Dean and Distinguished Professor of Law,
University of California,
Hastings College of the Law

LARRY D. KRAMER
Dean and Professor of Law, Stanford Law School

JONATHAN R. MACEY
Professor of Law, Yale Law School

WAYNE R. LaFAVE
Professor of Law, University of Illinois

ARTHUR R. MILLER
Professor of Law, Harvard University

GRANT S. NELSON
Professor of Law,
University of California, Los Angeles

JAMES J. WHITE
Professor of Law, University of Michigan

LEGAL, LEGISLATIVE, AND RULE DRAFTING IN PLAIN ENGLISH

By

Robert J. Martineau
Distinguished Research Professor of Law (Emeritus)
University of Cincinnati

Michael B. Salerno
Former Principal Deputy
California Legislative Counsel Bureau

Legislation Clinic
University of California, Hastings College of the Law

AMERICAN CASEBOOK SERIES®

THOMSON
™
WEST

Mat #40247695

Thomson/West have created this publication to provide you with accurate and authoritative information concerning the subject matter covered. However, this publication was not necessarily prepared
by persons licensed to practice law in a particular jurisdiction. Thomson/West are not engaged in
rendering legal or other professional advice, and this publication is not a substitute for the advice of
an attorney. If you require legal or other expert advice, you should seek the services of a competent
attorney or other professional.

© 2005 Thomson/West
      610 Opperman Drive
      P.O. Box 64526
      St. Paul, MN 55164–0526
      1–800–328–9352

Printed in the United States of America

ISBN 0–314–15301–2

TEXT IS PRINTED ON 10% POST
CONSUMER RECYCLED PAPER

To my children and grandchildren

—*Robert J. Martineau*

To my children, Gian and Giuliana
and in memory of Bion M. Gregory

—*Michael B. Salerno*

*

Foreword

Legal, Legislative, and Rule Drafting in Plain English is a substantially expanded version of Professor Martineau's Drafting Legislation and Rules in Plain English, published over a decade ago. Because of the book's history, this foreword supplements the original preface, which still applies and immediately follows. The expanded coverage acknowledges the common aspects of all legal drafting and includes drafting private legal documents in addition to legislation and rules, the focus of the earlier book. It also provides an orientation for drafting legal documents in general, and specifically legislation.

The new book's co-author, Michael Salerno, has over 30 years of practical drafting experience, having served as a consultant to both houses of the California Legislature and as a principal deputy in the California Legislative Counsel Bureau. He has taught as a visiting professor at the University of California Davis School of Law, was a Fulbright Scholar (Rome, 1995), and currently teaches at, and supervises a legislation clinic for, the University of California Hastings College of the Law.

Like its predecessor, this book is designed for both classroom use and as a manual for anyone who does any type legal drafting, both lawyers and non-lawyers. It may now be used in courses on legal drafting generally, in addition to courses on legislation that includes legislative drafting. It is also designed to be a reference guide when drafting legal documents. The book specifies drafting principles, provides examples, and gives advice on how to proceed before the drafting begins, such as how to elicit information from a client and the uses of forms. It explains the legislative process, the legislative drafting process, the special requirements for preparing a bill, the interrelationship between bill drafting and statutory construction, and includes administrative and court rule drafting. As in the previous book, the relationship between style and substance is stressed.

While writing is a skill that most acquire during general education, being able "to write" or even write well, does not translate into being able to draft legal documents. Legal drafting is a type of writing quite different than most other forms of writing. This book is not about general writing although much of the guidance it provides applies to all writing and will improve the ability to convey thoughts in written form. However, some of the principles will not improve all forms of writing. Other forms of writing, such as creative writing or a law review article, have different goals and must meet different demands such as keeping the reader's interest. Generally, the goal of legal drafting is not to compel the reader to turn the page. The reader of a legal document is interested in the substance of the writing without inducement. Legal drafting is not creative writing in the sense that literature is creative writing. "What does that passage mean to you?" may be an interesting question in a literature course; it is problematic in a legal document. The goal of legal drafting is not to entertain but to inform in a precise manner easily understood in the same way by all those who read the text. This book provides an approach to enable the legal drafter to attain that goal.

Professor Martineau wishes to acknowledge the valuable contribution of his son, Robert J. Martineau, Jr., in preparing Chapter 15, Allene Grognet, vice president (emeritus), Center for Applied Linguistics, for her helpful suggestions on the text, and Connie Miller of the University of Cincinnati College of Law's word processing department for her assistance in preparation of the manuscript and guiding us in the intricacies of word processing.

Professor Salerno wishes to acknowledge Avinash Kar, his principal research assistant who provided invaluable assistance, especially with the instructor's manual ands appendix of examples; his wife, Kathleen Turney, for lending her always helpful editorial skills; the students in his 2004 and 2005 Legislation Clinics for their comments and criticisms of the book; the University of California Hastings College of the Law, specifically his colleague Professor David Jung and Dean Mary Kay Kane, for their financial and personal support; and the Legislative Counsel of California, Diane Boyer-Vine, for her support encouraging his academic pursuits, although no part of this book reflects an opinion of the California Legislative Counsel Bureau.

ROBERT J. MARTINEAU
MICHAEL B. SALERNO

May, 2005

Preface to Drafting Legislation and Rules in Plain English

During my legal career my interests have concentrated on the fields of judicial administration, the appellate process, state and local government, and legislative and rule drafting. In my academic career I have limited my scholarship to the first three topics. I have, however, continued my drafting activities for a variety of groups and have taught legislative and rule drafting both as a full time academic and as an adjunct faculty member. My reasons for both engaging in legislative and rule drafting and teaching it to law students are the same—it is one of the most important things a lawyer can do while at the same time it is one of the most professionally satisfying. It is important because few things a lawyer does have a quicker and broader effect than drafting a constitutional amendment, statute, charter, or ordinance, or an administrative or court rule. Court decisions, by contrast, are far more likely to affect only a limited number of persons and in only limited ways. Drafting legislation and rules is professionally satisfying not only because it is important but also because it is a skill that can be developed, its development can be observed, and its effect is often readily apparent. Just as important is the satisfaction a writer feels in taking ideas that are vague, half thought out, contradictory, and even unexpressed and turning them into a law that is clear, concise, and substantively logical and consistent, not to mention socially useful. Seldom does the practice of law give so direct an opportunity to turn language into action, at least in the public arena.

The drawback to both the doing and the teaching, however, has been the lack of single text that included both an overall approach to legislative and rule drafting, explained the drafting environment for each, and developed specific drafting principles that would provide the drafter with a ready made style for most problems faced in drafting legislation or a rule. In particular, there was no text that combined the best of the principles of legislative drafting with the principles of the Plain English movement into a simple, usable guide for the legislation or rule drafter both in the classroom and in the "real world." The purpose of this book is to fill that void.

The title of this book includes the term "legislation." I interpret this term broadly to include constitutional provisions, charters, statutes, and ordinances as enacted by referendum or a legislative body. A legislative body includes, of course, Congress and state legislatures, but also city and county councils or boards of commissioners or supervisors. In addition, many other local governmental units such as townships, villages, towns, special districts, and authorities have legislative authority. Each adopts legislation, thus making the principles stated in this book applicable to the drafting of legislation adopted by each.

This book is equally applicable to rules. Who adopts rules? The obvious answer is federal and state agencies. To some, the regulatory age in which agencies do most of the law making through rules has superceded the age of statutes announced by Guido Calabresi only a decade ago. But these observers are concerned primarily with rule making by federal agencies and only to a limited extent by state agencies. The rules of these bodies, however, are merely the tip of the proverbial iceberg. There is even more rule making by local governmental agencies responsible for areas such as health, welfare, education, water and sewer, transportation, zoning, and planning, among others. Within each of these areas there are separate institutions, offices, and departments that themselves adopt rules. A university is a good example. It has rules for its governing board. Beneath it is the central administration divided into administration and academic affairs and each in turn is subdivided. For administration there are subunits for finance, budget, planning, personnel, facilities, safety, traffic, and athletics, just to name some. On the academic side there is the provost, graduate and undergraduate divisions, colleges, schools, and departments, not to mention service units such as hospitals. Each of them can and does have rules that govern the conduct of faculty, staff, students, applicants, patients, and committees in a variety of activities. Each group or subgroup or each activity can have its own set of rules. The combined product of all of these bodies is a staggering number of rules that must be drafted, read, understood, interpreted, and applied in thousands of instances every day. Again, the drafting approach and principles I have expounded in this book are as applicable to these rules as to legislation.

The intended audience for this book is anyone who drafts any type of legislation or rule I have just listed. For this reason it is not limited only to lawyers. While they draft much of the legislation and rules, by no means do they draft all of them. The drafter who is a non lawyer can benefit from this book just as much as the lawyer.

As with almost every published work, I could not have written this book without the assistance and advice of many others. Friends and colleagues who read drafts of some or all of the chapters are John Applegate, Kenneth Dau-Schmidt, Lynn Marmer, Ralph Towne, and Barbara Watts. Barbara McFarland not only made many useful editorial comments but also very helpful organizational suggestions.

I am particularly pleased to have my son, Robert J. Martineau, Jr., write the section on administrative rule making. It is a subject about which I know little and he knows much, and I was happy to benefit from his expertise.

My research assistants on this book, Pam Amlung and Betty Zea, each made a substantial contribution. In addition Betty Zea compiled the enacting clauses in Appendix B. They also prepared the initial draft of the exercises which will be published separately.

I owe a special debt to by students in my legislative drafting course in the spring semester of 1991. They were forced to struggle with an earlier draft of the manuscript. They not only did so with good cheer, but pointed out both typographical and textual errors. They were also of great help in the development of the exercises.

Lynn Clark and Connie Miller of the Word Processing Center at the College of Law and my secretary Melissa Wehmeyer labored exceedingly well under great pressure not only to type the text but to prepare it in camera ready copy.

To Dean Joseph P. Tomain of the College of Law I am indebted not only for financial support and released time to permit the book to be completed in less than one year, but for reading the manuscript and making a substantial number of worthwhile suggestions.

As always, the support and encouragement I receive from my wife, Connie, made it much easier for me to complete a project such as this.

Needless to say, errors still in the text are my sole responsibility.

ROBERT J. MARTINEAU

April, 1991

*

Table of Contents

*

The Hatter opened his eyes very wide on hearing this; but all he said was "Why is a raven like a writing desk?"

"Come, we shall have some fun now!" thought Alice. "I'm glad they've begun asking riddles—I believe I can guess that," she added aloud.

"Do you mean that you think you can find out the answer to it?" said the March Hare.

"Exactly so," said Alice.

"Then you should say what you mean," the March Hare went on.

"I do," Alice hastily replied; "at least—at least I mean what I say— that's the same thing, you know."

"Not the same thing a bit!" said the Hatter. "Why, you might just as well say that 'I see what I eat' is the same thing as 'I eat what I see'!"

Lewis Carroll
Alice's Adventures in Wonderland (1865)

*

LEGAL, LEGISLATIVE, AND RULE DRAFTING IN PLAIN ENGLISH

*

Part I

POOR LEGAL, LEGISLATIVE, AND RULE DRAFTING: THE PROBLEM AND THE CURE

Chapter 1

THE CAUSES OF POOR
LEGAL DRAFTING*

Lawyers are subject to criticism for many reasons, some justified and some not. One of the criticisms most prevalent, and at the same time most justified, concerns lawyers' writing skills. A text on legal writing summarized the results of a survey of persons familiar with legal writing in these terms:

> They think modern legal writing is flabby, prolix, obscure, opaque, ungrammatical, dull, boring, redundant, disorganized, gray, dense, unimaginative, impersonal, foggy, infirm, indistinct, stilted, arcane, confused, heavy-handed, jargon-and cliche-ridden, ponderous, weaseling, overblown, pseudointellectual, hyperbolic, misleading, in civil, labored, bloodless, vacuous, evasive, pretentious, convoluted, rambling, incoherent, choked, archaic, orotund, and fuzzy.

> Many critics have amplified: Lawyers don't know basic grammar and syntax. They can't say anything simply. They have no judgment and don't know what to include or what to leave out.[1]

Another author put it more simply: "Lawyers have two common failings. One is that they do not write well, and the other is that they think they do."[2]

There have been a number of efforts to explain the reasons behind this sorry state of affairs. The Goldstein and Lieberman text offers 14 separate causes of poor legal writing, from sociological ("every profession needs its own symbols and codes to set it apart from the rest of the world") to intellectual ("lawyers don't think clearly enough").[3] Richard Hyland places the blame for poor writing primarily on the inability of lawyers to think clearly rather than on an inability to write clearly.[4] The chairman of a state bar association committee offered four reasons for the failure of his group's drive to eliminate legalese in documents drafted

---

* Although the title of this book distinguishes between legal, legislative, and rule drafting to emphasize that it is concerned with the drafting of both private and public legal documents, for the purposes of brevity the text when referring to all three types of drafting will use only the term "legal drafting."

by lawyers—ignorance, apathy, stubbornness, and misrepresentation—which he called the "four horsemen of legalese."[5] Reed Dickerson wrote in 1954 that almost all lawyers and law professors consider themselves "well-trained, and even expert draftsmen."[6] Further, he noted that most see little inadequacy in other lawyers and law professors. They do not see a problem and, consequently, have no responsibility to solve it.[7] Our own experience of more than 30 years each of drafting state constitutional provisions, state statutes, city charters and ordinances, and court rules has persuaded us that Dickerson understated the problem. We have served with hundreds of legally trained legislators, lawyers, and law professors in various drafting environments. Of these, only a few have ever confessed and inability to draft any type of legal document. All, not just most, of the others firmly believe that they are expert drafters, and that the drafting abilities of other lawyers and law professors are fungible. To confess an inability to draft, apparently, is to declare oneself incompetent as a lawyer. To suggest that another lawyer or law professor is a poor drafter is to accuse that person of incompetence in a basic lawyering skill most assume all lawyers and law professors possess.

Some negative comments on the quality of legal writing in general have been directly toward the quality of the drafting found in legislation and rules. While it is likely that this increased focus is largely attributable to the ever increasing number and complexity of statutes and rules that govern our lives, the poor quality of legislative and rule drafting has not gone unnoticed over the years. A negative comment on the drafting of statutes made by Thomas Jefferson in 1817 is often quoted.[8] Jimmy Carter based his campaign for the presidency in 1976 partly on the complexity of the Internal Revenue Code. When president, he issued an executive order mandating the use of Plain English in rules adopted by federal agencies.[9] Rudolph Flesch, one of the founders of the Plain English movement, based his first book in 1946, as well as his most recent book in 1979, on the incomprehensibility of federal administrative rules,[10] and President Clinton issued an Executive Directive in 1998 to the same effect. Similarly, the drafting of English statutes has had critics as far back as the 16th Century. Edward VI asked for statutes to be "more plain and short, to the intent that men might better understand them."[11] A governmental commission in the mid 1970's made a comprehensive study of the drafting of English statutes. The first deficiency found was language. It quoted the Statute Law Society as saying that the language of statutes was "legalistic, often obscure and circumlocutious, requiring a certain type of expertise in order to gauge its meaning. Sentences are long and involved, the grammar is obscure, and archaisms, legally meaningless words and phrases, tortuous language, the preference for the double negative over the single positive abound."[12] By comparison with the attacks on legal writing in general, however, few of the critics have focused on legislative and rule drafting.

Several justifications can be made to explain this lack of attention. One is that legislative and rule drafting comprises a very small and specialized portion of all of the legal writing in which lawyers engage. In addition, in many states a few staff lawyers in the legislature's drafting agency draft most bills, thus even more sharply limiting the number of lawyers who draft legislation. Third, the principles that govern drafting legislation and rules are not different from those that govern other types of legal drafting, so no special attention need be given to it. Significantly, Reed Dickerson replaced his 1954 book The Fundamentals of Legislative Drafting in 1965 with The Fundamentals of Legal Drafting. Last, many consider poorly drafted legislation and rules the products primarily of legislators and bureaucrats rather than lawyers and thus not legal drafting in the sense of drafting done by lawyers. Even those who recognize the increased importance of legislation and have called for greater attention to be given to it in the law schools have concentrated on the study of legislation already adopted rather than the drafting of it.[13]

In fact, these arguments do not justify the apparent lack of concern for the inability of most lawyers to draft legislation and rules that are easy to read and easy to understand. The reality is that most legislative and rule drafting is done by lawyers. No matter what the makeup of the body adopting legislation or a rule, almost invariably its drafter is a lawyer. Further, legislative and rule drafting is not simply just another form of legal drafting. It is by far the most difficult because of the complexity of the problems it addresses, the vagaries of process by which its product is adopted, the unknown nature of its audience, and the permanency of its product.[14] The importance of legislation and rules can hardly be overemphasized. They control virtually every aspect of modern day life. Guido Calabresi has correctly pointed out that we now live in the Age of Statutes.[15] By this phrase he means that most law is now being made by legislatures and administrative agencies. Courts spend more and more of their time interpreting and applying legislation and rules than developing the common law.

Whatever the validity of the arguments, they do help explain why little effort has been made to improve the quality of drafting of legislation and rules even though the importance of legislation and rules has dramatically increased. They do not explain, however, why the drafting is so poor.

For many years one of the most dramatic examples of the lack of awareness by judges, lawyers, and law professors of the principles of good legislative and rule drafting is the U.S. Judicial Conference's Standing Committee on Rules of Practice and Procedure and its advisory committees. These committees are composed of some of the country's finest judges and most prominent lawyers and law professors. They do an excellent job of reviewing and revising the rules that govern practice and procedure in the federal courts. The rules they propose, however, consistently ignore not only the generally accepted rules of legislative and rule drafting as developed over the past half century by Dickerson and others, but also principles of good writing championed by Strunk and White and Flesch and good legal writing by Dickerson and Wydick.

A typical example of an advisory committee's work was a proposed amendment to Federal Rule of Evidence 404(b) concerning the admissibility of evidence of crimes, wrongs, or acts of a person. The then current rule provided that the evidence was not admissible to show character, but was admissible for other purposes such as to prove motive. The Advisory Committee on the Rules of Evidence proposed and the Supreme Court adopted and amendment that required the prosecution in a criminal case to provide the accused upon its request with advance notice of the general nature of the evidence it intends to introduce. In the classic style that has been decried by virtually every writer on legislative drafting, the Advisory Committee added the language as a proviso to the last sentence of the 404(b) as follows:

(b) Other crimes, wrongs, or acts. Evidence of other crimes, wrongs, or acts is not admissible to prove the character of a person in order to show action in conformity therewith. It may, however, be admissible for other purposes, such as proof of motive, opportunity, intent, preparation, plan, knowledge, identity, or absence of mistake or accident, <u>provided that upon request by the accused, the prosecution in a criminal case shall provide reasonable notice in advance of trial, or during trial if the court excuses pretrial notice on good cause shown, of the general nature of any such evidence it intends to introduce at trial</u>. [New material underscored.]

Starting with a sentence of 25 words, the amendment added the proviso with 48 words, thus making a sentence of 73 words. The proviso actually covers two situations—when pretrial notice is necessary and when the evidence is admissible without the notice. This suggests that the proviso should not only be a separate sentence but divided into two sentences. The first sentence should specify when the prosecution must give notice and the second what the court may do when the prosecution does not comply with the first sentence.

The proviso has other problems. It refers to *"notice in advance of trial"* and *"pretrial notice"* when it means the same thing. It refers to *"any such evidence"* when *"the evidence"* would be sufficient. It refers to *"reasonable notice"* and then defines the notice to be given as notice of *"the general nature"* of the evidence to be introduced, thus making it unclear whether the term *"reasonable"* applies to the nature of the notice or to when it is given. Also unclear is whether the authorization to the court to allow the evidence at trial if good cause is shown applies only when the accused has made a pretrial request for notice with which the prosecution has not complied. If so, the evidence is presumably admissible without court approval if no pretrial request has been made. If not, court approval is required even when no pretrial request is made. Another question, one that goes to the substance of the rule and not to drafting style and which would have been highlighted by proper drafting, is why the prosecution should be required to give pretrial notice only if the accused requests it. Obviously, the prosecution knows if it intends to introduce the evidence, but the accused does not. If the evidence is admissible without notice unless a request for notice is made by the accused, in every case the accused will be forced to make a request, thus further increasing the flow of paper in every case. Far simpler would be to put the burden on the prosecution to give the pretrial notice when it knows in advance that it intends to introduce this type of evidence, but upon a showing of good cause to permit the court to allow the evidence if pretrial notice has not been given.

To avoid all of these problems, the proviso should be a separate sentence and read:

> *In a criminal case, the prosecution shall give notice a reasonable time before trial of the general nature of the evidence it intends to introduce. If the prosecution fails to give the notice, the court may admit the evidence if it finds good cause for the failure.*

There was no excuse for such poor drafting, but there is an explanation: the persons who serve as reporters for the Advisory Committees and do their drafting are experts in the substantive areas covered by the rules, not in drafting legislation or rules. Furthermore, the members of the committees are concerned with the substance of the rules and not with drafting style. The result was poorly drafted rules that created problems for litigants, their attorneys, and the judges who interpret and apply the rules.

The good news is that the Standing Committee recognized the problem had its Subcommittee on Style engage Professor Bryan A. Garner to develop Guidelines for Drafting and Editing Court Rules published in 169 FRD 176 (1997). These guidelines were used in the revision of the Federal Rules of Appellate Procedure adopted in 1998 to make the rules simpler to read and easier to understand. Unfortunately, these guidelines have not been used for the revision of any of the other federal rules of practice and procedure.

The situation is even worse in the legislative and administrative rule areas. In some jurisdictions the staffs of individual legislators, legislative committees, and legislative drafting agencies draft most legislation. It is often the case that, other than possibly the head of a legislative drafting service, none of these drafters is likely to have had any specialized training in legislative drafting. The staff members of individual legislators and legislative committees are mostly young professionals with political connections, political ambitions, or both, but no training or expertise in drafting. If they become expert in anything, it is in a substantive area of the law, not in drafting. The staff members of legislative drafting agencies are again likely to be young lawyers, few who are specially trained in drafting or who develop an expertise in drafting .. They are under pressure to produce many bills on a whole variety of subjects in a very short time, which does not enable them to become expert in either a substantive area of the law or in drafting. The adoption of term limits in some states has further exacerbated the problem because it has resulted not only in a more rapid turnover of legislators, but also in their staffs, thus losing the benefits of any training in drafting they may have received. The staffs of administrative agencies that draft rules are similar to the staffs of legislative committees—experts, if at all, on substance, not drafting.

Endnotes

1. T. Goldstein and J. Lieberman, The Lawyer's Guide to Writing Well 3 (2002).

2. Felsenfeld, The Plain English Movement in the United States, 6 Canadian Business Law Journal 413 (1981–82).

3. Goldstein and Lieberman, supra note 2 at 18–19. The other 12 are:

*Professional. Lawyers are trained to be exhaustive researchers.

*Competitive. The competitive society demands prolixity.

*Legal. The law requires "legalese."

*Economic. Lawyers make more money by writing poorly.

*Historical. Creatures of precedent, lawyers do what was done before, solely because it was done before.

*Ritualistic. People must believe in the majesty of the law, embodied in its ritualistic language.

*Technological. Modern machines such as the typewriter are responsible.

*Institutional. The pressure of business is responsible.

*Deterministic. The way lawyers write is the best way to accomplish the law's goals.

*Pedagogical. Lawyers never learned to write well.

*Cultural. Lawyers don't read enough or know enough of their heritage to write better.

*Psychological. Lawyers are afraid to reveal themselves.

4. R. Hyland, A Defense of Legal Writing, 134 U. of Pennsylvania L. Rev. 599, 621 (1986).

5. Hathaway, The Plain English Movement in the Law, Past, Present and Future, 35 Michigan Bar Journal 1236, 1237 (1985).

6. R. Dickerson, Legislative Drafting 3–4 (1954).

7. Id.

8. "I should apologize, perhaps, for the style of this bill. I dislike the verbose and intricate style of the modern English statutes. . . . You however can easily correct this bill to the taste of my brother lawyers, by making every other word a "said" or "aforesaid" and saying everything over two or three times so as that nobody but we of the craft can untwist the diction, and find out what it means." Letter to Joseph C. Cabell, Sept. 9, 1817, in 17 The Writings of Thomas Jefferson 417–18 (Lipscomb ed. 1905) quoted in D. Mellinhoff, The Language of the Law 253 (1963).

9. 10 Executive Order No. 12044, Mar. 23, 1978, 43 C.F.R. 12661.

10. R. Flesch, The Art of Plain Talk, 164–71 (1946); R. Flesch, How to Write Plain English (1979).

11.   Quoted in The Preparation of Legislation ¶ 2.8, Command Document 6053 (1975).

12.   *Id.* at ¶ 6.3. For a further discussion of the situation in England see M. Zander, The Law Making Process 23–35 (5th ed. 1999).

13.   One effort was R. Posner, The Problems of Jurisprudence 262–85 (1990). He stated his current view on legislation as well as lists of works of others in Posner, Legislation and Its Interpretation: A Primer, 18 Nebraska L. Rev. 431 (1989). His call for greater attention to be given to legislation in law schools was made in Posner, Statutory Interpretation—In the Classroom and in the Courtroom, 50 U. of Chicago L. Rev. 800 (1983). The most widely used book used in law school courses on legislation, W. Eskridge and P. Frickey, Cases and Material on Legislation in its 2001 edition devoted only 12 of a total of 1195 pages to legislative drafting.

14.   In 1955, Reed Dickerson pointed out that "legislative drafting is the most difficult form of legal drafting. The basic problems are the same but legislative problems are technically more complicated and socially more important." Dickerson, How to Write a Law, 31 Notre Dame Lawyer 14, 15 (1955).

15.   G. Calabresi, A Common Law for the Age of Statutes (1982).

Chapter 2

HOW TO IMPROVE THE QUALITY OF LEGAL DRAFTING: THE RELATIONSHIP BETWEEN STYLE AND SUBSTANCE

Identifying a problem and its causes is often relatively easy but finding and implementing a solution is much more difficult. In the case of legal drafting, the problem of poor drafting and its causes are detailed in chapter 1. The thesis of this book is that the application of the drafting principles set forth in it, principally in chapters 5–9, can eliminate or substantially reduce most of the problems of poor drafting. Our philosophy, developed in our more than 60 years combined experience drafting legislation and rules and teaching law students how to draft them, is that following the principles of drafting style set out in this book is the best way to produce good legal drafting that is both sound in substance and easy to understand. We recognize that this statement is directly contrary to the traditional advice given to legislative and rule drafters to concentrate on substance first and leave style to a cleaning up process. Our experience, however, has been that if the drafter is concerned initially with substance, postponing attention to style until the substance is agreed upon, the result will be a document, legislation, or rule that is neither well thought out nor well expressed.

Essentially, this approach to legal drafting is an application of the principle that writing is the best test of thinking. Arthur Littleton made this point when he wrote "language is something more than a tool of thought. It is a part of the process of thinking."[1] Our corollary to the principle is that structured writing is the best way to force structured thinking. Substantive analysis and the writing process do not occur in consecutive order, with the writing following the analysis. Instead, they occur concurrently, with the writing driving the analysis as much as the analysis drives the writing. The use of drafting principles from the first step in the process imposes a discipline on the analysis that produces not only language that is simpler and more easily understood but also a solution to the problem that is itself less complex and more easily understood. Following the drafting principles set forth in this book will not only make the legislation or rule drafted in accordance with them clearer and more easily understood, but also accomplish the substantive goal the proponent seeks to achieve. To put it in more common terms, clarity of expression is more likely to produce clarity of thought than the latter is likely produce the former.

Over the past 50 years, separate but overlapping efforts have been made to improve legal writing and to professionalize legislative and rule drafting. A special development has been the Plain Language (often called Plain English) movement, directed primarily at making legal documents drafted by lawyers, particularly those that affect consumers such as insurance and installment contracts as well as government regulations, easier to read and understand. During the past two decades a substantial number of states enacted "Plain English" statutes, mandating the use of simplified language in these types of policies and contracts. Some statutes directed government agencies to draft their rules and regulations in accordance with the same principle. More recently, some authorities have recommended Plain Language for legal writing in general. A few have suggested that legislative and rule drafting could benefit from the application of Plain Language principles, but no one has yet made a comprehensive effort to combine the best principles of legislative and rule drafting with those of the Plain Language movement to apply to all legal drafting. The authors believe that by building upon the work of Strunk and White, Flesch, and Wydick on the Plain Language side and Dickerson on the legislative drafting side, it is possible to develop principles for all legal drafting in simple, clear, and understandable language. Those principles are set forth in chapters 5–9.

The Plain Language approach to legal writing in general and to legislative and rule drafting in particular is not without its critics. Veda Charrow has attacked some of the premises of the Plain Language advocates, including those that maintain that short sentences, short words, common words, and avoidance of the passive will necessarily result in writing that is clearer and thus more easily understood.[2] More specifically, Professor Frank Grad, long time director of Legislative Drafting Research Fund at Columbia University Law School, challenged the relevance of Plain Language to legislative and rule drafting. He says that Plain Language is a false issue and that he does not even know what it means. He defended complicated language and complicated statutes in the following terms:

> Many problems that need legislative resolution are complex and difficult . . . We need complex language to state complex problems of law or fact. . . . I simply assert that here, too, form follows function. The language of drafts of legislation should address itself to the problem to be resolved. If complex problems require complex language for their resolution, so be it. No trained draftsman will use complex forms of expression unnecessarily. . . . [3]

In the past decade several articles in the Statute Law Review and a book by two staff members of legislative services, one American and one British, have challenged the validity of the Plain Language movement as the solution to the problems of poor legislative and rule drafting. Their position is that Plain Language principles do more harm than good because they do not take into account the complexity of drafting legislation and rules in the modern world. Rather than focusing on the reader, as does the Plain Language movement, good drafting principles should focus on the drafter. Similarly, the goal of good drafting should be accuracy, not clarity.[4] It is significant that this same resistance has not been found in other areas of legal drafting. For example, the Securities and Exchange Commission in 1998 amended its rules relating to corporate prospectuses to require that they be written in Plain English with no objection from those who must prepare the documents.[5]

Again, the authors' own experiences in legal drafting prove exactly the opposite. Contrary to Professor Grad's position, in legal drafting, style (form) is not merely a product of function. Rather, style and function each develop simultaneously, with each having a major impact on the other. Perhaps even more important is to determine exactly what is the function of the legislation or rule. The function is twofold—to solve a problem and to do so with language that is readily understandable by those who are affected by it or who must administer it. The resolution should be as simple as the value of the problem allows, expressed as clearly and concisely as possible. As to both, the style becomes part of the function and is inseparable from it.

Professor Joseph Williams has pointed out that there are three things to understand about complex writing: it may precisely reflect complex ideas or it may gratuitously complicate either complex ideas or simple ideas.[6] Style, if used as part of the drafting process, can not only avoid the last two but also help to reduce if not eliminate the first.

The role of the drafter of legal document is very similar to that of the appellate advocate. In writing a brief, the best advocate is the one who can take a long and complicated set of facts and organize and relate them in such a way that the facts are easily understood by the readers of the brief. In addition, the advocate must reduce all of the possible issues in the case to one or two issues, each of which can be set forth in a statement of the question presented. The statement must include the key facts in one sentence of reasonable length, which is easily understandable on the first reading. The whole purpose is to take what appears long and complicated and reduce it to what is concise and clear. The task of the drafter of a legal document is exactly the same. A brief that is too long and complicated cannot be justified by the argument that facts and issues in the case are long and complicated. The same principle applies to any legal document, public or private. For this reason style—the principles expressed in this book, including Plain Language—is also important in legal drafting.

Of course, simply having principles of drafting is not itself sufficient to guarantee that a document, legislation, or rule will be easy to read and understand. The principles must be designed to produce legal documents that are clear and easily comprehensible. The Plain Language movement can make a substantial contribution to the effort to improve the quality of the legal drafting. The Plain Language approach forces the drafter to focus on the audience of the document. As expressed by a Canadian bar and banker's committee, "[p]lain language drafting is a form of writing that focuses on the needs of the reader."[7] Every provision in a document, legislation, or rule is designed to result in action or to have a legal effect. To the extent that the audience of a document, legislation, or rule has difficulty in understanding it, the likelihood it will accomplish what its drafter intends is reduced. The goal of Plain Language is to minimize this risk. Identifying the audience and selecting words to accommodate that audience are discussed in chapter 8, section B.

This book can, of course, only set out the drafting principles the authors believe are correct and have found helpful in their drafting experiences. Actual improvement in the quality of the legal drafting will occur only if those who do the drafting learn and follow these principles. This will depend on the extent to which the principles are taught to law students and others who engage in legal drafting. This in turn will depend upon whether those for whom legal drafting is done understand the importance of drafting principles and insist that those who draft for them know and comply with the principles. If private clients, legislators, judges, and heads of administrative agencies continue to be concerned only with substance and to ignore style, the quality of legal drafting is not likely to improve.

Endnotes

1. Littleton, The Importance of Effective Legal Writing in Law Practice, 9 Student Lawyer 6 (1963).

2. V. Charrow, What is "Plain English" Anyway? 2–10 (Publication C 1, Document Design Center, American Institutes For Research, 1979) reprinted in R. Dickerson, Materials on Legal Drafting at 278–82 (1981).

3. Grad, Legislative Drafting as Legal Problem Solving—Form Follows Function, In Drafting Documents in Plain English 481, 489 (Practicing Law Institute, Commercial Law and Practice Course Handbook Series No. 203, 1979) reprinted in R. Dickerson, Materials on Legal Drafting 277 (1981).

4. J. Stark, The Art of the Statute (1996); Hunt, Plain Language in Legislative Drafting: Is It Really the Answer?, 23 Statute L. Rev. 24 (2002); Stark, Should the Main Goal of Statutory Drafting Be Accuracy or Clarity?, 15 Statute L. Rev. 207 (1994).

5. 17 CFR 230.421. See also SEC Release No. 33–7497 (01/28/1998). The SEC also issued a Plain English Handbook (1998) to guide the preparers of corporate documents.

6. J. Williams, Style xi (1990).

7. Canadian Bar Association and Canadian Bankers' Association Joint Committee on Plain Language, The Decline and Fall of Gobbledygook: Report on Plain Language Documentation 1 (1990). The report uses the term "plain language" rather than "plain English" because, of course, of the bilingual makeup of Canada. The report was published in English and French.

*

Part II

SETTING THE STAGE

Chapter 3

FINDING OUT WHAT THE CLIENT WANTS AND TRANSLATING THOSE DESIRES INTO A LEGAL DOCUMENT

A. COLLABORATIVE PROCESS

Legal drafting is a collaborative process between the client and the drafter. The degree of collaboration is determined by the sophistication of the client, the clarity of the request, the complexity of the assignment, the drafter's knowledge of the substantive area of law, and the drafter's experience. The drafter should know that writing is a process, and there is more than one approach to that process. This chapter contains one suggested approach. There are many other approaches that basically address the same issues.[1]

B. DRAFTER AS ARCHITECT, BUILDER, AND JOURNALIST

A "classic analogy" aptly describes the legal drafter's role as that of both architect and builder.[2] While the client may know what is desired as the end result, it is the task of the drafter to determine whether that result is possible and, if so, how it may be accomplished. It is the drafter's role to attain the goal of the client and, consequently, the first step in the drafting process is to lay a foundation by determining precisely what the client desires.

A legal drafter can also benefit from the advice given journalists. Before writing a news story, a journalist must know the "who, what, where, when, why, and how" of the story. The same is true with legal drafting. The drafter plays a role similar to a journalist when interviewing a client. It is essential the drafter gather as much information concerning the facts and circumstances surrounding the particular request in order to address the legal issue or issues that will be contained in the legal document. As in most aspects of practicing law, preparation is a critical element.

C. KNOW THE LAW

The value the legal drafter adds to the process of reducing a person's desire into a legal document is several fold: the drafter determines whether the goal is achievable, where there are limitations or barriers to reaching the goal, and the approach to accomplishing the achievable result.

Before meeting with a client it is essential that the legal drafter know the general law that relates to the legal drafting assignment.[3] This knowledge should include more than the substantive and procedural aspects of the particular area of law. The drafter should also be familiar with judicial decisions interpreting the law. A drafter does not need an encyclopedic knowledge of all law. In a modern practice, with the increasing complexity of law and the tendency for specialization, the general practitioner is a vanishing breed. Specialization occurs even within specific fields of law. A client who desires a contract to be drafted is unlikely (nor would be well advised) to consult with someone who specializes in litigation. A contract for the purchase of goods or services differs from a contract for the purchase of real property. While wills and trusts might fall within the rubric of "family law," it is doubtful a specialist in drafting wills would draft a complex document in connection with the dissolution of a marriage, even though divorce is a subcategory of family law. If the drafter does not have at least a basic knowledge of the area of law governing a legal document, it must be acquired because without this knowledge, it is difficult, if not impossible, to produce a legal document that meets minimum professional standards.

The acquisition of this basic knowledge should occur before meeting with the client, although usually a preliminary communication or meeting with the client is necessary to determine the broad areas of law implicated in the request. Even a drafter who possesses a detailed knowledge of the particular area of law may determine after meeting with the client that additional research is needed.

D. KNOW THE AUDIENCE

It is essential that the drafter "know the audience." This is to say that, in addition to being aware of the goal of the client, the drafter should have familiarity with the party or parties on the other side of the table as well as how a dispute will be resolved should one arise after the document is in force. Obtaining information, whether anecdotally from others who have dealt with the party or by searching public records, is often helpful in anticipating issues that may arise in connection with the document and to avoid unnecessary points of dispute. It is also helpful to determine the economic or political power of the other parties when anticipating remedies.

Attention should also be directed to the forum in which a dispute will be resolved should one arise. For example, should the instrument call for arbitration or mediation in lieu of judicial resolution of a dispute? If a dispute concerning the document is likely to be resolved in court, how long will it take to resolve the matter in that forum? Can an alternative venue more favorable to the client be specified? While these strategic decisions will ultimately be based on the client's desire and the extent to which the other party is amenable to alternative approaches, the drafter should raise them during the drafting process. The drafter needs at least this basic information to assist the client in making the most prudent decisions.

With respect to drafting legislation and rules, knowing the audience is a bit more complex because of the political nature of the task, and the bifurcated life of legislation or a rule, first as a bill or draft rule, subject to amendment, and then, as a statute or rule with an entirely different audience (see chapters 10, 11, 14, 15, and 16).

E. DETERMINE THE GOALS OF THE CLIENT

Obtaining from the client a clear explanation of what is desired is essential to the drafting process. The first step in this process often involves determining whether the client has a clear understanding of the goal of the document, which should never be assumed.[4] Often, the client interview and the presentation and discussion of the request for a legal document will help the client in further defining what is desired. It is at this time the legal drafter relies on both legal and interpersonal skills in eliciting from the client the intended goal of the document.[5] In most cases, based on a general knowledge of law, the drafter will have a better sense than the client of whether the requested outcome is feasible. With respect to drafters and the increasing specialization of modern legal practice, a legal drafter who has an expertise in a particular area of law will be better able to assess the client's problem, elicit the necessary information, and provide alternative solutions for the client to consider. For example, an attorney who practices family law will have a reservoir of legal knowledge not only of the basic parameters of child custody law and judicial preferences where the attorney practices, but also the tax consequences of an agreement that ends a marriage. While the client may have a clear idea of the desired result, it is the drafter who can determine whether the result is obtainable and what, if any, obstacles are presented.

The objective of the legal drafter's meeting with the client is to gather all the necessary facts the client knows and to determine whether additional information is necessary. It may be necessary to ask the client to provide additional information. The form in which the client delivers the information is also important. The client should be told that assisting the drafter by thoughtfully organizing and indexing the materials the drafter is required to review will have an impact on the amount of time it will take to complete the request.

It is often suggested that a legal drafter prepare a checklist or inventory to assist in gathering the information necessary to draft a product that clearly addresses the objective of the client. The nature of the checklist or inventory will be dictated by the drafting task. Unfortunately, it is not possible to create a universal approach because drafting tasks differ from one area of law to another. If the drafter were drafting a trust, the questions asked would be quite different from the questions asked if the task were to prepare a commercial lease. The information needed to prepare a contract is quite different from the information needed to draft a complaint. It is for this reason, among others, that the novice drafter, or the drafter embarking on an new area of law, might find use of a commercially drafted form quite helpful in preparing a checklist or inventory (forms are discussed at greater length in chapter 4).

Taking the example of drafting a commercial lease, the following checklist or inventory specifies some, but not all, of the information that the drafter may need to elicit from the client:

1. Description of property to be leased

2. Names of lessor and lessee

    Point of contact for notice between lessor and lessee

3. Term of the lease

    Option to renew

    Early termination

4. Rent amount

    Move in allowance

    Due date of first payment

    Due date of periodic payments

    Penalty for late payment

    Discount for prepayment

    Inclusion of services, utilities and supplies

5. Occupancy

    Early occupancy

    Late occupancy

    Holding over

    Remedy if occupancy is not possible on the date of lease

    Condition that premises must be delivered

    Condition that premises must be maintained

Condition that premises must be surrendered

Responsibility for maintenance and repair

Discovery of a dangerous condition after occupancy
   (e.g. presence of asbestos or other toxic materials)

Alterations to premise

6. Purpose of possession

   Requirement for quiet possession

   Restrictions on use of premises

7. Consent to assign and sublet

8. Inspections

9. Insurance

   Subrogation and indemnity

10. Destruction of premises by event beyond control of lessor/lessee

Because the drafting process actually begins with the initial client contact, the drafter should use this initial contact to elicit as much information as possible about the legal problem and what the client wishes. The acquisition of this knowledge can start with a broad conversation about the legal problem and be followed up by a more specific session where the legal drafter raises a series of questions. It is at this time that the drafting process becomes a collaborative one, with the client explaining the nuances of the problem and the drafter explaining the legal alternatives. Through this dialogue the client learns more about the complexity of the ultimate goal, the legal drafter helps the client in sharpening focus on what is feasible, and in identifying limitations or alternatives, and the task becomes refined.

The complexity of the task, the experience of the legal drafter, and the sophistication of the client will determine if one conversation or more is necessary before actually starting to write the document. The client may not know the answer to critical questions and may be asked to gather additional facts. Based on the client's explanation, the legal drafter may be required to do additional legal research. It is the drafter's goal to prepare competently the document, which requires the drafter will "know the problems in detail, foresee the pitfalls, bring these to the client's attention, and present relevant choices that the client must sooner or later make."[6]

An important element of the client interview process is conveying to the client the time it will take to complete the requested task. The ability to accurately analyze how much time a given project will consume is a skill developed over years of practice. However, following the principle that a task generally takes longer than anticipated, the drafter should give the client a clear idea of how much time (the number of hours) the final product will require, perhaps favoring a higher rather than a lower estimate or presenting a range that will depend on specified factors, such as the ability of the client to provide relevant documents or the amount of legal research that may be necessary prior to drafting. The drafter should be prepared to justify the amount of time predicted by explaining the complexity of the request. Generally, a novice drafter will bill for fewer hours than are spent at a task because some of this time is really attributable to the drafter's education. In other words, a novice drafter may decide to bill only for the number of hours it would take a seasoned drafter to draft the same document. After acquiring a bit of experience, the number of hours a legal document takes to draft and the number of hours the drafter will bill become closer to the same number.

F.   PREPARE A PLAN

Once the goal of the client has been clarified, it is often helpful to develop what Dickerson calls a "plan of organization,"[7] that is a very detailed outline to assist the legal drafter in first establishing an inventory of what is needed in the document and to provide a framework for the final product. Many drafters use the checklist created for the client interview in tandem with, or as a basis for, the plan for the legal document.

The plan should be a road map that considers all aspects of the drafting task. Once again, there is no uniform format. The plan will be dictated by the nature of legal document and the particulars of the client's goal.

It is important to note that the preparation of the plan assumes the legal drafter "knows the law" which, as indicated above, is the first step in the process of legal drafting. It also assumes the drafter has a clear idea of the goals of the client. At this stage, the drafter has identified the important legal concepts that will be the basis of the document. As the plan emerges, the drafter will review the plan to determine if it is comprehensive. Does the plan address all of the issues that are necessary to resolve? Are the issues presented in a logical and coherent fashion? Are there legal or logical gaps in addressing any legal issues? Does the plan contain any unnecessary parts that are duplicative, contradictory, or inconsistent with other parts of the plan? In addressing these questions, the drafter may discover a need for answers to questions that were not apparent when the client was interviewed. It is also common for the drafter to determine that there are legal issues requiring additional research.

The plan should also include an estimate of how much time each component will require as well as the time necessary to complete a first draft. The amount of time needed to turn the first draft into the final product will depend on the quality of the first draft and factors that are not necessarily within the drafter's control, such as the time it will take colleagues to review the draft.

G. FIRST DRAFT AND ITS REVISIONS

Drafting the document is not a one step process even after the legal drafter has all the information necessary to start writing. Except for the most simple of legal documents and the most experienced drafter, the first draft is just what its designation implies, a first attempt at crafting the legal document. The degree of perfection a drafter might achieve is a function of both time available for the task and the expense the client is willing to incur. Much legal drafting, especially legislative drafting, is done under extreme time pressure.

There is no simple formula on how to draft. The drafter must simply begin to write, keeping in mind the principles set forth in this book and following the plan that the drafter has developed. It is through the process of actually writing that the drafter either validates the plan of organization or determines that the plan has flaws. The drafter should never be unwilling to revise the plan if the need arises.

The drafter should be prepared to write and rewrite the "first draft" several times. A dozen revisions of the "first draft" are not uncommon before the drafter has a "first draft" suitable to submit to the next step in the process. The drafter may find it useful to prepare an overall first draft that covers the entire document, but is not a detailed draft, to determine if the plan is coherent and complete, and then, to work back through the document filling in the details. Many drafters find it helpful, after working though a rough draft from beginning to end, to subdivide the document into logical parts and work on perfecting the component parts as separate mini-tasks. This approach is especially helpful in drafting a complex document because it divides what may seem like a daunting job into smaller, more manageable parts.

The technology associated with writing has provided better tools to the drafter. Most drafters use a word processor. Word processing allows the drafter to move effortlessly around words, phrases, and sentences to make them fit in a more logical sequence. It also allows the drafter to maintain multiple versions of a draft in chronological order by saving them as Draft 1, Draft 2, etc. Computer technology allows the drafter to review the document several times searching for particular terms to ensure consistency. Finally, it is now possible to compare easily one draft with another by using a program for that purpose.

Once the document is complete, the drafter should review it several times in to ensure that proper grammar is used and the other principles of this book are observed. It is also useful to refine the language in the document. A very helpful suggestion made by Richard Wydick is to review the draft to omit surplus words. He recounts a story from the time he was a young lawyer, about a more senior attorney who "hated verbosity" and would take what was considered a finished product and "strike out whole lines, turn clauses into phrases, and turn phrases into single words."[8] As the drafter works through the document with the goal of eliminating verbosity, the product that emerges is a cleaner, crisper version of the initial draft.

It is often helpful, if time permits, to set the document aside once the drafter is satisfied that a first draft is acceptable and to work on other projects. This breather from the drafting assignment can range from a few hours to a day or two. Setting the draft aside gives the drafter the ability to read it again with a fresh perspective. It is generally surprising how a document prepared on one day and thought of as acceptable will have problems when read at a later time.

Before the drafter is satisfied with the first draft, it should be checked to make sure that it satisfies four criteria: the document is clear, consistent, non-duplicative, and contains all necessary components.

H.   SHOW THE DRAFT TO COLLEAGUES

Perhaps the greatest "sin" associated with all forms of writing, but especially critical to avoid in legal drafting, is the sin of pride. There should be little, if any, pride of authorship concerning the first draft of a legal document. As mentioned earlier in this book, each author has over 30 years of legal drafting experience. Neither has ever prepared legal document that was not improved by having it reviewed by colleagues. Having at least one other set of eyes look at the first draft and suggest ways in which it can be improved is an indispensable step in the drafting process.

The colleague who reviews the draft should be an individual with comparable, if not greater, drafting experience. That colleague need not know the law or even what the client has requested, although that information may be provided to the reviewer. It is the role of the person who reviews the document to draw attention to errors in the draft, such as grammatical problems, missing words, problematic organization, the omission of necessary provisions, gaps in logic, and verbosity. Most importantly, the reviewer should convey to the drafter what the draft means to the reviewer and whether the drafter's intent is clear to the reviewer. There is no better way of determining whether the draft achieves its goal of stating the client's desire. If the reviewer has to ask the question, "What did you intend?" or "Did you mean this or did you mean that?" in any part of the draft, the drafter must revisit the provision and clarify it.

The drafter must avoid being defensive when the first draft is returned with the reviewer's comments, questions, and suggestions. This is not to say the drafter should blindly accept the reviewer's conclusions, but if another person reads the work product and raises concerns, those concerns should be at least considered, and addressed if necessary, in a subsequent draft.

I. THE FINAL DRAFT

The term "final draft" is not synonymous with "final document." It simply denotes that the drafter is satisfied with the document and it is ready to be shown to the client. The final draft may be the final document. The final draft may require half a dozen or more revisions. The true test of the final draft is when the client reads and agrees with the product. The greater the sophistication of the client, the more likely the draft may need further refinement. This need for further refinement is not necessarily a negative outcome. As mentioned early in this chapter, the legal drafting process is a collaborative one. The client and the drafter share the same goal. It is always satisfying to have the client simply smile and say, "This is exactly what I wanted." However, it is sometimes more helpful if the client raises questions and informs the drafter that one aspect or another of the document is not really what was intended and identifies aspects of the document that do not meet the client's goals. It is much better to have this feedback before the writing becomes a final document, is used, and a dispute subsequently arises.

Endnotes

1. See D. Cohen, Competent Legal Writing—A Lawyer's Professional Responsibility, 67 U. Cin. L. Rev. 491 (1999), footnote 35:

> "Writing is a process. Although the labels may vary from writer to writer, there are steps to the writing process that include understanding the substance, identifying the audience for the document, organizing the substance, expressing the substance in writing, and editing and revising the writing.

2. The "notion that the draftsman of a statute is both its architect and its builder is not new."

The drafter is the first person, after the client, to be actively engaged in the project and from the very outset must know the client's objective.

The drafter must:

> "determine the specific need;"

> "the relationship of new building to existing buildings;"

> "study materials, construction, and form of the related buildings so that the new structure "both in the need it serves and in the architectural style to which the institution is already committed;"

> "relate [to client] "things that are legally permissible in that area" such as the code, zoning limitations, restrictive covenants, need for permit;"

> organize "the elements into a concrete whole that will give the client the greatest service with the least expense, inconvenience, and compromise;" and

> "fit the whole into an appropriate artistic pattern and to add those stylistic configurations that will make the building an acceptable aesthetic experience to those who work in it or have to look at the outside;"

An architect "must participate in exploring the objectives, sketch the structural framework, fill in the broad surfaces, work out the significant detail, and add aesthetic touches." R. Dickerson, Legislative Drafting 11–12 (1954).

3. In some instance, the drafter may not know the subject before meeting with the client, in which case unless the drafter is an expert in the particular area of law, the drafter can simply gather the facts concerning the clients request and determine whether a subsequent meeting is necessary after the drafter has the opportunity to research the law.

4. "The client has rarely thought the problem through or even considered all the relevant factors." R. Dickerson, Legislative Drafting 14 (1954).

5. "[D]rafting calls for the highest in tact and flexibility" R. Dickerson, Legislative Drafting 150 (1954).

6. R. Dickerson, Legislative Drafting 14 (1954).

7. R. Dickerson, The Fundamentals of Legal Drafting 59 (2d ed. 1986).

8. Richard Wydick, Plain English for Lawyers 9 (4th ed. 1998).

Chapter 4

USE OF FORMS

A. FORMS IN GENERAL

A legal drafter should know about the existence of forms, their advantages and disadvantages, and the value of creating the drafter's own forms. There are several types of forms.[1] To name just a few, there are commercial forms in all areas of law[2] (such as wills and trusts) forms prepared by business organizations (such as a "model lease") and public forms created by bar associations, courts, or court agencies that are used for pleadings and discovery.[3] In the field of legislative drafting there are model acts.[4] Existing law and previously introduced legislation can also be used in a manner similar to forms when drafting statutes. The comments in this chapter are general and may not apply to all forms.

B. A WARNING

First, a caveat: As Ruta K. Stropus stated in an article entitled, "The Art of Drafting":

> "Beware of forms. There is no need to reinvent the wheel every time you draft a document. Exercise caution, however, when using forms or other reference documents. Forms are often written in legalese and may not convey ideas clearly and precisely. By blindly incorporating form language into a new document, you not only perpetuate poor writing, you risk miscommunicating your client's intentions. The forms found in form books are, by necessity, broad and vague. They are intended to reflect the needs of some artificial "composite" client rather than one with specific, unique needs." [footnotes omitted] [5]

With that warning in mind, a legal drafter should not hesitate to consult or use a form <u>as a reference or starting point when drafting</u>. But a form should not be used with confidence as printed unless it is an official form created by a court for a particular purpose.

The legal drafter who makes use of a form must first overcome what Sidney Saltz called the "psychological barrier to critical judgment ... created simply by the fact that a document has been printed."[6] As Saltz advises, "The drafter should be aware of this barrier not only when reviewing a form to be used in drafting but also in reviewing another lawyer's draft that appears to be on a preprinted form."[7]

C. WHAT IS WRONG WITH FORMS

A legal drafter should be aware that forms vary in quality. Some forms are quite good and drafted in a style consistent with the legal drafting this book advocates. Other forms are drafted in an arcane style and can be vastly improved. Forms are helpful tools, but present basic problems.

First, there may be problems with the style in which forms are written. Forms often use arcane language, indefinite adjectives, compound constructions or expressions, run-on sentences, redundant legal phrases, and lawyerisms. A poorly drafted legal form can provide an excellent drafting exercise. Simply take the form and edit it, applying the principles of this book. Three results will follow. The length of the document will be greatly shortened. The document will become easier to read. The purpose of the document will become more apparent. If the style of forms were the only problem with using forms, then the solution would be simple and contained in this paragraph. Unfortunately, there is more to what is wrong with forms.

Second, forms are usually general in nature. They may not recognize statutory or decisional law in the jurisdiction in which the form is used. The form drafter may be from another jurisdiction and may not address the special considerations the law of your state requires. What may be considered an adhesion contract in California may be perfectly acceptable in another state. A provision that is void against public policy in New York may be the public policy of another state. The form drafter seldom includes in an appendix a multi-state disclaimer or index identifying how the form applies to the various jurisdictions in which it may be used. A form found in a formbook was drafted for "every-client," not your client. The person who drafted the form has never met, much less interviewed, your client. The form drafter has no knowledge of the unique facts and circumstance your client presents and cannot meet your client's goal, unless the request is truly generic.

Third, the form may contain errors. The error may be in the form as first drafted. The error may have developed as the law changed and the form aged. A proper statutory citation may be accurate one year and wrong in a subsequent year. A recent court decision may make an entire clause in a form either obsolete or inaccurate. Worse, the retention of language in the form drafted before the decision may nullify the favorable application of the decision to your client. For example, a court decision may provide that as a matter of law a particular public policy that favors your client applies unless a provision in the contract provides to the contrary. Using a form drafted prior to this decision that includes the provision contrary to the new statement of public policy would defeat your client's interest. Forms do not carry malpractice insurance to cover errors, whether inherent in the first draft or due to a change in the law after the form was printed.

Fourth, forms tend to favor one-side of a legal agreement. Continuing with the example of a commercial lease used in chapter 3, this point is apparent when examining most forms for leasing of real property, which generally favor the lessor. If a legal drafter were drafting a commercial lease on behalf of a lessee, the drafter should not rely on a commercial lease form as the basis of the lease.[8]

Finally, forms can be both over-inclusive and under-inclusive at the same time. Depending on the particular legal drafting goal and the particular form consulted or used as a template for drafting, it is likely the form will contain elements that have no application to the task at hand. At the same time, it is likely the legal drafter may be required to supply additional language to adequately address the issues presented by the drafting task.

D. HOW TO USE FORMS

Given the numerous and somewhat daunting limitations of forms, one might question their use. But even those who advocate "original drafting" concede their usefulness if "used sparingly and properly— never in lieu of your own thinking."[9]

Using a form can save the legal drafter a considerable amount of time compared to "starting from scratch." The better the form, the more likely it will expedite the drafting process. When addressing a drafting task in an area new to the legal drafter, it may be helpful to consult more than one formbook to determine which is best suited to the assignment and to possibly use different parts from more than one form.[10] At a minimum, one or more forms can be the basis of an outline.

One advantage of consulting a form is that another legal drafter has thought generically about the issue and has usually spent a considerable amount of time crafting the form. The form has likely gone through numerous iterations and will, at a minimum, draw to the drafter's attention many of the issues associated with the drafting task. A form may also draw to the drafter's attention issues that had not been considered prior to reviewing the form. For example, a contract between two parties residing in different states requires a choice of law clause that sets forth the jurisdiction and the manner in which disputes will be resolved or a liquidated damages clause. These types of details may not occur to the novice drafter, but may be standard provisions in a form.

While a form may have inadequacies, it can provide guidance, especially for the novice legal drafter as a starting point and tool. A form can identify many of the basic issues that must be addressed in the instrument requested. A form can also assist the drafter in creating a checklist for the client interview, and a preliminary outline for the instrument. If the form is well written, or can be redrafted to be well written, it may be used as a template for the actual draft, requiring only that it be supplemented and tailored to the particular drafting task.

The goal of the legal drafter in working with a form is to make the form the drafter's own. A drafter who begins with a particular form, revises that form to be consistent with the principles of preferred legal drafting, consults with other forms and perhaps borrows additional provisions or language, and adds new provisions applicable to the jurisdiction in which the drafter practices, will soon have a product that is a reflection of the drafter's work.

After this initial work, the legal drafter will gain confidence in the customized form and may use it for other assignments with less need for modification. It is common for a legal drafter who works in a law firm to use forms developed by others in the firm for similar legal documents. The drafter realizes the reward of efficiency, the tremendous amount of time saved by using these customized forms after the basic work is completed. Nonetheless, regardless of how comfortable a drafter is with a form that the drafter or other lawyer in the firm has created, it is still necessary to reevaluate the form for changes in law that have occurred since the form was last used and to alter the form to apply to the particular nuances of the drafting assignment at hand.

Endnotes

1. "Usually forms are available from a variety of sources. There are formbooks galore. There are forms drafted by bar associations, title companies, banks, trade associations and legal form companies." S. Saltz, Drafting Made Easy, 15 Probate & Property 32, 34 (May/June, 2001).

2. There are 30 volumes of forms published by West ranging from five volumes relating to business organizations to four volumes of specialized forms.

3. For example, the California Judicial Counsel provides a variety of forms, some required by statute, which are available on line, go to: http://www.courtinfo.ca.gov/forms/.

4. For example, the National Conference of the Commissions on Uniform State Laws, founded in 1878, drafts uniform acts and promotes them (see G. Grossman, Legal Research, Historical Foundations of the Electronic Age 181–187 (1994)).

5. See Stropus, The Art of Drafting, 83 Ill. B.J. 543 (1995).

6. See S. Saltz, supra, note 2.

7. Ibid.

8. Although in this example, a commercial lease form is useful to highlight what the lessee does not want in the lease or the terms and conditions that should be revised to make them favorable to the lessee.

9. L. Brody, J. Rutherford, L. Vietzen, and J. Dernbach, Legal Drafting 18 (1994).

10. Brody et al. uses the analogy of the drafter as a master chef and the forms as recipes, to which the drafter "refers to from time to time for ideas." However, this analogy stresses that the chef must be familiar with the "effect of each ingredient" to know how to revise the recipe to make the final product "delectable for each customer's particular tastes." Ibid.

*

Part III

DRAFTING PRINCIPLES

Chapter 5

CONCENTRATE ON THE WHO
AND THE WHAT

The purpose of a private legal document, legislation, or rule is to impose a burden or confer a benefit, not to be merely descriptive. When the drafter attempts to determine what that result should be and to accomplish that result through the use of language, the first principle that should guide the drafter is to concentrate on the "who"—the person on whom a legal burden is imposed or benefit is conferred, and the "what"—the burden imposed or benefit conferred. The actor is the who; the action and the object or the complement are the what. In terms of sentence structure, the who—the actor—is the subject of the sentence, and the what—the action and the object or complement—is the predicate. The primary responsibility of the drafter is clearly to identify both. If the drafter fails in this responsibility, a reader of the document, legislation or rule will be uncertain about its intended effect, and a court will then have the opportunity to construe the document, legislation, or rule in a way not intended by its proponent or the parties, legislature or agency signing or adopting it.

Clarity of expression is only one reason to concentrate on the who and the what. Just as important is for the drafter to think through clearly what it is that the document, legislation, or rule is designed to accomplish. Seldom will the client for whom the drafter is preparing a document, legislation, or rule have more than a rough idea of what it should include. Even less likely will the proponent have thought out its details. The drafting of a document, legislation, or rule does not merely express the previously formed intent of those for whom the drafter is working. Only in the drafting is the client's intent developed. At this stage of the drafting process, almost every word chosen by the drafter reflects a policy choice. In some instances the client will previously have made those choices and informed the drafter of them. In most instances the number of choices the client or drafter must make becomes apparent only in the drafting process. The drafter must first either consult with the client or choose a word that reflects a choice and then bring it to the attention of the client, explain the alternatives and why the drafter selected the one reflected in the draft, and then be directed by the choice made by the client.

Drafting thus becomes not merely the process by which words are chosen to reflect choices previously made, but, as is explained in chapter 2, the process by which the range of choices is identified and one of the alternatives selected. Focusing on the who and the what is the best means to accomplish this process of identification because these are the substantive elements of the document, legislation, or rule. Because of their importance, they serve as the organizational structure for explaining and demonstrating the principles of good drafting in chapters 6–9.

Implicit in the thrust of this chapter as well as chapters 6–9 is the use of the active voice. Although the active voice is not discussed until chapter 7 because it relates to the action, if importance were the organizational basis for these chapters, the active voice would be discussed first. When the drafter uses the active voice, most of the other drafting principles set forth in chapters 6–9 become much easier to understand and to follow.

Chapter 6

THE WHO—THE ACTOR

A. USE THE SINGULAR*

A traditional principle of legal drafting is to make the subject of a sentence singular rather than plural. When combined with the direction to use the active voice, this means that the actor in each sentence will be singular.

Use of the singular is important for several reasons. First, the singular makes the drafting process simpler because there is no need to worry about accidental shifting back and forth between the singular and plural in nouns, pronouns, or verbs. Second, the singular particularizes the effect of the provision being drafted on the individual rather than on the more anonymous group. Third, the singular makes it clear that the provision applies to each member of the class rather than only to the class as a separate group or body.

Even though proponents of good legal writing have long advocated use of the singular, drafters of legislation and rules still use the plural to an astonishing degree. This may be because the drafter fears that using the singular will cause courts to find that some person or entity intended to be covered by the provision is not covered. This fear is unwarranted. To say *"a"* or *"an"* is not the same as saying *"one,"* and courts do not so hold. One of the reasons for this is that the Model Statutory Construction Act of 1965 in section 3 and its successor, the Uniform Statute and Rule Construction Act of 1995 in section 6.5 state that the singular includes the plural (and vice versa). The annotations to these sections indicate that this provision is found in the statutory construction acts of all but a few states.

An example of the unnecessary use of the plural can be found in 28 U.S.C.A. § 41. It reads as follows:

---

* For chapters 6, 7, and 8 there are in the appendix examples of poor drafting and proper drafting that supplement the examples given in the text.

Special sessions of the district court may be held at such places in the district as the nature of the business may require, and upon such notice as the court orders. (38 words)

Using the singular and the active voice, the section would read:

Upon notice, the district court may sit any place in the district. (11 words)

Dickerson suggests that if it is necessary to use the plural, the drafter can change to the singular by first using the plural, and then saying "*such a* _____." He uses the following example:[1]

Employees who have earned 15 or more point credits are eligible for positions under section 9. <u>Such an</u> employee....

There are two problems with this example. First, there is no reason to use the plural. Both the subject of the sentence, "*employees,*" and the object, "*positions,*" should be stated in the singular as follows:

An employee with 15 or more point credits is eligible for a position under section 9.

The next sentence can then begin "*The employee ...*"

This change eliminates the second problem with Dickerson's recommended draft, the use of the prohibited "*such.*"

B. IDENTIFY THE ACTOR

Many documents, legislation, and rules, but especially legislation and rules, offer many examples the imposition of a command that an action be taken without clearly specifying who has the duty to take the action. While the actor can often be inferred from the text, it is preferable specifically name the actor. For example proposed legislation may seek to prevent an intoxicated person from receiving a marriage license. Instead of drafting a provision that states that *A marriage license may not be issued to a person who is intoxicated,* the drafter should determine who issues marriage licenses and name that person in the legislation. The provision should thus read *The County Clerk may not issue a marriage license to a person who is intoxicate (or an intoxicated person).*

Use "*a person*" to designate the actor in the provision unless there is some reason to limit the application of a provision in a document, legislation, or rule to a designated class. This term is the most general because it covers both natural and artificial persons and all types of entities no matter what their formal legal status. Section 26(4) of the 1965 Statutory Construction Act defined "*person*" to mean "*individual, corporation, government or governmental subdivision or agency, business trust, estate, trust, partnership or association, or other legal entity.*" The annotation to the section states that this definition is taken from the Uniform Commercial Code and that most states adopted similar provisions. The 1995 Act is to the same effect. If the persons or body that will enact legislation or adopt a document or rule has not elsewhere adopted a definition of person, the document, legislation or rule will have to include one. Do not use what might be thought of as synonyms for *"person,"* such as *"individual," "party," "body,"* and the like. The synonyms can only create doubt as to how broadly the provision is intended to apply.

Often, of course, a document, legislation, or rule will apply only to certain classes of persons. There are two ways to limit the applicability of a provision. One is to use a term that carries the limitation as part of its meaning (*child* or *minor* to mean a person under age 18 or *attorney* to mean a person admitted to the practice of law). The other is if the actor is referred to only once or twice, the term *"person"* with the qualifier should be used. If the actor is referred to more often, then the term that contains the qualifier in its definition can be used, but only if the term is defined in the definition section of the document, legislation or rule so that there is no doubt as to its meaning (see chapter 8, section A on definitions).

The need for consistency, discussed in chapter 8, section E, is particularly important in references to the actor. For example, in 28 U.S.C.A. §§ 2241–55, a person seeking a writ of habeas corpus is referred to as a *"prisoner,"* a *"person in custody,"* a *"person detained,"* a *"petitioner,"* and an *"applicant"* in various places in the sections. Presumably all references are to the same person, but only confusion can be created by the use of five different terms to refer to the person seeking the writ.

C.   USE ARTICLES AS MODIFIERS

1.   Use *"A"* or *"An"* Rather than *"Any," "Each," "Every,"* or *"No"*

As discussed in the previous section, the term used to identify the actor is chosen to include all those intended to be covered by the provision, but no others. That term will be preceded by an article (*a* or *an*) or an indefinite adjective (*any, each, every,* or *no*). In almost every instance an article should be used (*a person, an applicant*) rather than the adjective (*any person, each applicant, every party*). For some reason, legal drafters tend to use the adjective rather than the article, presumably fearing that the courts will confuse *"a"* or *"an"* with *"one,"* and hold that the right or duty conferred by the document, legislation, or rule is applicable only to a single member of the class.

Do not follow the traditional advice that has recommended: (1) if a right, privilege, or power is conferred, use *"any"* (*any party may file a motion*); (2) if a duty is imposed, use *"each"* (*each appellant shall file a brief*); (3) if a right, privilege, or power is abridged, or an obligation to abstain from acting is imposed, use *"no"* (*no person may vote without first registering*).[2] The legal effect of a provision is exactly the same if *"a"* or *"an"* is used and *"a"* or *"an"* are shorter and simpler. In addition, confusion is created if an article is used in most places, but occasionally an adjective is used. A court or other person attempting to construe the provision may conclude that the different usage was intended to have a different meaning, even though it was used merely for emphasis.

If, of course, the provision is intended to apply to only one and not an indefinite number, then the use of *"a"* or *"an"* would be inappropriate. In those instances the adjective *"one"* should be used (*"the director may appoint one assistant"*).

Use of the adjective *"no"* is never proper with the actor (see chapter 6, section F and chapter 7, section A 6 for a discussion of the proper way to express the negative).

In a private legal document these rules may be inapplicable because the parties covered by the document may be identified. In this case "the" should be used (*the employee, the buyer, the lessor*). See section 2.

2.   Use *"The"* Rather than *"Such"* or *"Said"*

A favorite lawyerism is to use *"such"* or *"said"* as an adjective to identify a noun previously referred to (*A resident who registers is qualified to vote. Such (or said) resident may....*). Neither *"such"* nor *"said"* is necessary or proper. Use the article *"the"* instead (*The resident may....*). It conveys the same meaning and is less stilted. Use of a pronoun such as *"it," "they,"* or *"them"* may also be appropriate but only if the noun to which the pronoun refers is unmistakable. The adjectives *"that"* and *"those"* (*that applicant* or *those applicants*) should not be used because they add nothing to *"the."*

Sometimes *"such"* is used to suggest a choice (*the court may issue such orders as it considers appropriate*). Even then, the use of *"the"* is preferable (*the court may issue the orders it considers appropriate*). *"Such"* may be used, however, with *"as"* to list examples (*the applicant may file supporting documents such as a birth certificate, tax return, or driver's license*).

D.   LIMIT THE USE OF PRONOUNS

The drafter must be careful in the use of pronouns because of the possibility of ambiguity in the noun to which the pronoun refers. Consider the following provision.

> *The governor shall file a copy of the State's plan with the administrator. If he determines that the plan does not meet the requirements, he shall adopt a temporary plan for the State.*

In the second sentence, there are two *"he's."* The first *"he"* probably but not necessarily refers to the administrator. It is even more unclear, however, whether the second *"he"* refers to the administrator or the governor. To avoid this type of ambiguity, the second sentence should read, *"If the administrator disapproves the plan, the administra-*

tor shall adopt a temporary plan for the State." This sentence is longer than the original because "*administrator*" has more letters than "*he,*" but clarity should always prevail over brevity if there is a conflict.

Another reason to avoid the use of pronouns is to avoid the use of sexist language. Until very recently documents, legislation, and rules almost always used the masculine when an expression of gender was thought necessary. This occurred most often when a pronoun was used. "*He,*" "*his,*" or "*him*" was the standard; "*she,*" "*hers,*" or "*her*" were used only when the actor could not be a male. A problem of interpretation was handled by a rule of interpretation, usually incorporated into the first chapter of a code, stating that the masculine includes the feminine. The 1965 Model Statutory Construction Act in section 4 was more diplomatic. It provides that "words of one gender include the other gender." The 1995 Act is to the same effect. The use of the masculine to include the feminine is no longer acceptable. Some legislatures and rule drafting bodies have embarked on long term efforts to eliminate sexist references in previously adopted legislation and rules. Virtually all have agreed to adopt new legislation or rules that are gender neutral, unless a masculine or feminine reference is appropriate, such as when referring to a father or mother.

It is easy to adopt this principle, but somewhat more difficult to implement it. Wydick gives several rules appropriate for the legal drafter that he says "may help."[3]

One rule is to use gender neutral terms when you can do so without artificiality. The "*draftsman*" of a statute or rule has now become the "*drafter.*" In most states, "*workmen's*" compensation laws have become "*worker's*" compensation laws. Wydick also recommends against creating artificial terms such as "*waitperson.*"[4] Often a neutral term such as "*waiter*" is available. One chronic problem for legal drafters has been an acceptable alternative for "*chairman.*" Neither "*chair*" nor "*chairperson*" works well. Perhaps "*chairmember*" may be acceptable, or something completely different such as "*presider*" or "*presiding member.*"

The second rule is not to use gender based pronouns. Wydick has six suggestions for accomplishing this.[5] Two are useful for the legal drafter.

One is to omit the pronoun. Instead of saying "*a juror is entitled to $10 for each day he serves*" say "*a juror is entitled to $10 for each day served.*"

The other is to repeat the noun instead of the pronoun, as discussed earlier in this section.

To demonstrate these two techniques, take the sentence that in earlier times would have read "*an inventive drafter can always come up with a solution to any problem he faces.*" Under the first technique it would read "*an inventive drafter can always come up with a solution to any problem the drafter faces*" and under the second "*an inventive drafter can always come up with a solution to any problem faced.*"

Another technique is to use *"it"* when the noun antecedent can refer to an artificial legal entity such as a corporation or partnership as well as a human being. Thus if the antecedent is *"person," "party," "trustee," "employer," "taxpayer," "appellant," "owner," "tenant,"* or the like, *"it"* is just as appropriate as *"he"* or *"she"* and avoids the sexist objection. If, however, the antecedent can only be a human being such as *"driver," "drafter," "parent,"* or *"student,"* then *"it"* cannot be used.

E.   LIST OR CHARACTERIZE MULTIPLE ACTORS

If a provision is applicable to more than one actor, then the drafter must decide how to list them. If applicable to only two or three actors, they can be listed in a simple series (*a county, city, or town may issue bonds*). If, however, the list contains so many actors that the readability of the provision will be adversely affected (*a county, city, town, village, township, school district, special taxing district, water district, sewer district, park district, regional authority, park authority, or any other political subdivision of the state having taxing authority may issue bonds*) an alternative to the simple listing should be adopted. The first alternative is to list a single word that would include each member of the series, and then define the word to include all of the members. For the example just given, the term *"political subdivision"* would probably be appropriate. That term could be defined, and then the provision would read *"a political subdivision may issue bonds."*

Another alternative is to tabulate the series (see the discussion of tabulation in chapter 8, section G). Also discussed in that section is the proper use of *"and"* or *"or"* in a series. Whether *"and"* or *"or"* is used before the last word in a series, always use a comma before the next to the last in the series to avoid confusion as to whether the last two items in the series are separate or combined (*an officer, director, employee, and agent*). If the comma is not placed before the *"and,"* it is not clear whether the employee must also be an agent and an agent must also be an employee to be included. If the two are intended to be separate, the comma should be included. A drafter seeking clarity should ignore the advice of some grammarians that the comma is not necessary. This point is discussed in Lynne Truss' Eats, Shoots and Leaves at pp. 83–87.

F.   SAVE THE NEGATIVE FOR THE ACTION

One of the most common ways to express the negative in a document, legislation, or rule is to use a *"no"* as an adjective for the actor in the provision. The 14th amendment to the U.S. constitution, for example, provides that *"No State shall make or enforce any law which shall abridge the privileges or immunities of citizens of the United States."* An even more common expression, particularly in criminal statutes, is to say *"no person shall . . . ."* The purpose of these provisions is to prohibit the action specified. Dickerson points out that this form of expression means only that no one is <u>required</u> to act. But as he points out, it negates the obligation, but not the authority to act.[6] In its place, Dickerson recommends the use of *"no person may"* to express the prohibition.[7]

The principal error of the traditional form and Dickerson's suggestion lies in expressing the negative in the actor. Literally, a provision that begins with *"no person"* is not addressed to anyone, when the exact opposite is intended—the provision applies to everyone. The negative thus properly belongs with the action, not the actor. The proper way to express the prohibition is to say *"a person (or other actor) may not."* Thus, the prohibition contained in this section should not read *"no drafter shall use 'no' as an adjective to express a prohibition"* but should read *"a drafter may not use 'no' as an adjective to express a prohibition."* The latter not only is correct, it also reads better. For more on expressing a negative command, see chapter 7, section A 6.

Endnotes

1. R. Dickerson, Fundamentals of Legal Drafting 125 (2d ed. 1986).

2. Id. at 217; W. Statsky, Legislative Analysis and Drafting 184–85 (2d ed. 1984).

3. R. Wydick, Plain English for Lawyers 78–80 (4th ed. 1998). The effort to eliminate sexism is not without its critics. See R. Dickerson, Materials on Legal Drafting 186–93 (1981). For a more sympathetic view, see J. Williams, Style 194–95 (1990).

4. R. Wydick, supra note 3 at 75–76.

5. Id. at 66.

6. R. Dickerson, supra note at 215–16.

7. R. Dickerson, supra note 1 at 130–31.

Chapter 7

THE WHAT—THE ACTION AND OBJECT OR COMPLEMENT

A. THE ACTION

1. Use Active Voice

The most important legal drafting principle and the one upon which most of the others depend is the command to use the active voice. Its use is not merely to be preferred, as most others suggest. The principle is use the active voice unless it is inappropriate. Grammatically, active voice refers to the use of a transitive verb in a sentence. A transitive verb is one that requires an object to complete its meaning. To say that a verb is used in the active voice means that the subject of the sentence is the one who engages in the action described by the verb while the object of the verb is the result of the action. Thus if the verb is *"to write,"* the subject of the sentence is the person who writes while the object of the sentence is that which is written. The form of the verb is *"write"* or *"writes,"* depending upon whether the subject is in the first, second, or third person and singular or plural (*a party writes a brief* or *the parties write a brief*). The opposite of the active voice is the passive voice, in which the subject of the sentence is the result of the action described by the verb, while the actor is relegated to being the object of a preposition (*a brief is written by a party*) or not even mentioned (*a brief is written*).

The first and foremost reason why it is so important to use the active voice is because it requires the drafter to identify the actor. This is crucial in all legal drafting but even more important in drafting widely applicable documents, legislation and rules because of their very nature. Reed Dickerson has stated that "[l]egal drafting is the crystallization and expression in definitive form of a legal right, privilege, function, duty, status, or disposition."[1] He then points out that the main difference between legislation and rules on the one hand and private instruments such as contracts and wills on the other is "that the former are devoted almost entirely to regulating conduct or fixing a legal status, whereas many of the latter . . . are mainly dispositive."[2] Broadly applicable documents such as insurance policies, deed restrictions, and employee benefit plans are much more like private statutes because they primarily establish rights and duties for those who did not participate in drafting the document.

When a sentence in a document, legislation, or rule expresses a legal right, privilege, function, duty, or status (which we will refer to as a benefit or a burden), the active voice compels the drafter to identify the person or body that has the benefit or burden (*a corporation shall appoint an agent, a corporation may issue stock*). It is crucial that the drafter and the reader be made aware of who receives the benefit or the burden, because the "who" defines the precise parameters of the document, legislation or rule. The remaining words in the provision define the nature of the benefit or burden and consist of a verb and its object. They constitute the predicate of the sentence. The drafter can create few greater problems than to leave unclear who is the recipient of the benefit or burden of a provision in a document, legislation, or rule.

The active voice has another direct and immediate benefit—it forces the drafter to consider carefully the verb of the sentence that creates the benefit or burden. In determining how broad or narrow the benefit or burden should be, identification of its recipient is also crucial. The close relationship between the recipient and the benefit or burden means that the identification of the recipient is as much controlled by the expression of the benefit or burden as the benefit or burden is controlled by the recipient. Once the drafter chooses the words to identify the benefit or burden, the drafter may have to revise the description of the recipient so that: (1) the recipient and the benefit or burden are in accord with one another; (2) the document, legislation or rule reaches all those and only those it is intended to reach; and (3) it grants only that benefit or imposes only that burden it is intended to grant or impose.

The active voice has several other benefits. First, it usually requires fewer words. "*A taxpayer shall file a return*" has six words, but "*a return must be filed by a taxpayer*" has eight words. Second, it is easier to understand. Because it identifies the actor first, it uses the direct, shorter expression "*file*" rather than the more complicated "*be filed by,*" thereby using fewer words. Most experts on readability contend that the active voice usually makes language easier to read than the passive voice.

In a document, legislation, or rule, the action is never more important than the actor. By its very nature a document, legislation, or rule works only when it imposes a burden or benefit on a particular actor. The actor is, consequently, always as important as the benefit or burden. Although Wydick states that the passive voice does have some proper uses: (1) when the thing done is more important than the actor; (2) when the actor is unknown; (3) for emphasis at the end of a sentence; (4) when detached abstraction is appropriate; (5) when you want to muddy the waters intentionally.[3] None of the reasons applies to legal drafting.

As to the first, in a document, legislation, or rule, the action is never more important than the actor. The second permitted use of the passive voice, when the actor is unknown, again is inapplicable to a document, legislation or rule for the same reason—the recipient of the burden or benefit should always be known. If the recipient is unknown, the drafting is faulty. The best way to avoid this type of problem is to use the active voice. Using the passive voice for emphasis at the end of the sentence is also inappropriate in a document, legislation or rule. For the reasons just given, a provision should give equal emphasis to the actor and to the action because each is equally important. To emphasize one over the other is a mistake. Lastly, a document, legislation or rule is no place for detached abstraction or intentional muddying of the waters.

As noted at the beginning of this section, the active and passive voices come into play only when a transitive verb is used, a transitive verb being one that requires an object upon which to work (*an applicant shall submit two copies*). A variation of the active voice occurs when the verb is intransitive rather than transitive. An intransitive verb is most often used in a document, legislation or rule to connect the subject of a sentence to a noun, pronoun, or adjective (called a complement). Examples are to establish status (*a person under age 18 is a minor*), eligibility (*a person 65 years of age is eligible to receive benefits*), an entitlement (*a member of a board is entitled to be reimbursed for expenses*), or a penalty (*the penalty for violating section 467 is a fine of $1,000*).

In these instances, the active voice is not appropriate and the drafter should not use it. The drafter could convert a statement of eligibility, entitlement or sanction in which an intransitive verb is used into a sentence that uses a transitive verb (*the agency shall pay benefits to a person who is 65 years of age, the corporation shall reimburse a board member for the member's expenses, the court shall impose a fine of $1,000 upon a person convicted of violating section 467*). Focusing on the person who has the status, is eligible or entitled, or the violation for which the sanction is established usually is, however, simpler and uses fewer words.

2. Use Base Verbs

The use of a nominalization in place of a verb is a technique common to lawyers and bureaucrats. A nominalization is the creation of a noun out of a verb. The nominalization of the verb *"consider"* is *"consideration,"* *"decide"* is *"decision,"* *"determine"* is *"determination,"* *"file"* is *"filing,"* and *"accept"* is *"acceptance."* While nominalizations are not intrinsically wrong, the drafter should avoid using them in a document, legislation or rule. The nominalization is always a longer word than the base verb and the nominalization always requires supporting words, usually an article and a verb. Thus, a provision that with a base verb reads *"the administrator shall consider the application"* becomes with a nominalization *"the administrator shall give consideration to the application"* or *"the court shall determine"* becomes *"the court shall make a determination . . . . "*

The inevitable result of the longer and additional words is that the document, legislation, or rule is more difficult to read and to understand.

3. Use the Present Tense and the Indicative Mood

Two closely related problems in legal drafting are tense and mood. They are treated together here because they both involve the improper use of the word *"shall."* A verb can be in the past tense (*a court had jurisdiction*), the present tense (*a court has jurisdiction*), or the future tense (*a court will (shall) have jurisdiction*). The legal drafter is seldom tempted to use the past tense, but there is a strong temptation to use the future tense. The drafter quite naturally thinks in terms of the future because whatever is written today will almost always affect only events in the future. Even if the drafter thinks in terms of the action of the parties or legislative or rule making body, when the parties or body acts, it will do so on a particular day to control actions after that day.

Use of the future tense in a document, legislation, or rule is not correct because it ignores the principle that the document, legislation, or rule always speaks at the time it is applied to specific facts. For a document, legislation or rule, the time is always now for any operative provision. Absent a "sunset" provision, a document, legislation, or rule is effective for an indefinite period. During that period the document, legislation, or rule should read as though it had been adopted that very day and as though the adopting body were speaking directly to the reader at the very moment the document, legislation or rule is being read.

In addition, the present tense has several other advantages. It makes the document, legislation, or rule easier for the reader to understand, because there is no need to make the mental transfer from the future to the present tense. Use of the present tense will also make the document, legislation, or rule shorter because it uses fewer words than the future tense.

Seldom in legal drafting is the past or future tense appropriate. When the document, legislation, or rule describes a condition or event that precedes the operative provision, the past tense may but need not be used. If the condition or event comes after, use the future tense. The following example uses the past tense in the first clause and the future tense in the second. *"If a person has been convicted of a felony, the person will (shall) be ineligible to apply for a grant."* Both the past and future tenses can be eliminated by having the example read *"if a person is convicted of a felony, the person is ineligible to apply for a grant."* In most instances, use of the past or future tense can be avoided by careful drafting. In the example just given, the provision would be better if it read *"a person convicted of a felony is ineligible to apply for a grant."*

An even more common mistake in legal drafting is the use of *"shall"* or *"shall not"* to declare a legal result rather than to give a command. For example, the 1977 federal Clean Air Act provided in 42 U.S.C.A. § 7607(d)(7)(A) (1983) that *"The record for judicial review shall consist exclusively of . . . ."* In 28 U.S.C.A. § 1498(d) it provides that *"A Government employee shall have a right of action against the Government . . . ."* This usage is known as a *false imperative* because it does not give a command to someone to do something but rather declares a legal result. A document, legislation or rule is self-executing. If it says something *"is,"* it is. Thus, if in a document, legislation, or rule a word has a certain meaning, it is only necessary to say that the word *"means...."* This usage is the indicative mood. To say that a word *"shall mean"* is incorrect. Title 28 of the U.S. code repeatedly gives jurisdiction to federal courts by saying a court *"shall have jurisdiction"* when it should say a court *"has jurisdiction."* In the example from the federal Clean Air Act quoted above, the statute should read *"The record for judicial review consists exclusively of...."* The provision in 28 U.S.C.A. § 1498(d) should read *"A government employee has a right of action against the government."*

In addition to the use of *shall* in these circumstances being technically incorrect, the use of the indicative mood has two other advantages. Most important, it allows the use of *shall* only in those instances when the imperative mood is appropriate, that is when a command is given (see the discussion in chapter 7, section A 4). Elimination of the unnecessary *shall*, of course, also reduces the number of words in the provision.

4. Use *"Shall"* Only to Impose a Duty to Act

As discussed in chapter 7, sections A 3, 5, and 6, the legal drafter should not use the word *"shall"* to indicate the future tense, the false imperative mood, to impose a duty not to act, or to impose a limitation. That leaves only one use for *"shall,"* to impose a duty to act. The provisions *"the president shall report annually to congress,"* *"the governor shall submit a balanced budget to the legislature,"* *"a person shall pay a tax each year,"* *"an attorney shall keep client funds in a separate account"*, and *"the seller shall repair the automobile without charge"* are all examples of commands for the actor named in the provision to take an action. Some authors have opted for the use of *"must"* rather than *"shall"* to impose a duty, arguing that the various ways in which *"shall"* has been used has so corrupted it that it should not be used at all. We disagree, believing that its traditional use as the imperative is both traditional and proper.

The action to be taken can be ministerial, that is it does not involve the use of discretion (*the clerk shall enter on the docket the filing of a pleading in a case*). The action can also involve the use of discretion such as preparing a balanced budget or filing a report. The ministerial act can be directly enforced by a writ of mandamus if a public official is involved or an action for specific performance for a private party. A discretionary act is not enforceable by mandamus or specific performance but is subject only to a variety of indirect enforcement procedures such as impeachment or removal from office for a government official, or a criminal sanction, contempt of court, or an administrative penalty for an official or private party. In some instances, the duty may be unenforceable either directly or indirectly by legal means. The obligation thus becomes only a moral or political obligation. If a constitutional provision on initiative or referendum directs that *"the legislature shall adopt laws to implement this section"* the only sanction on members of the legislature who fail to enact the legislation is the possibility that voters may vote against the legislators at the next election. The duty to act is, however, no less a duty.

In two types of provisions the use of *"shall"* appears to be appropriate but is not. The first is when a provision imposes an obligation by stating that an act must be done in a certain manner (*a pleading shall be filed with the clerk*). *"Shall"* also appears appropriate when a limitation is imposed on a discretionary act or a grant of authority (*an aggrieved party shall file an appeal within 30 days of entry of judgment* or *the governor shall fill the vacancy from a list of three persons nominated by the commission*). These uses of *"shall"* are incorrect because they appear to create a duty to act when none exists. In the examples given, an aggrieved party is not required to file a notice of appeal, it is only required to act within 30 days if it chooses to appeal. Similarly, the governor is not required to fill the vacancy but is limited to the list of nominees if the position is filled. (If the intent is to impose a duty to fill as well as to limit the choice to the list of nominees, the duty to fill should be stated separately from the limitation.) There are two ways to give discretion or authority, and then to impose a limit on it. One is to express the grant of discretion or authority in terms of a qualifying statement (*to appeal a final judgment an aggrieved party shall file a notice of appeal within 30 days of entry of judgment* or *to fill a vacancy, the governor shall appoint one of three persons nominated by the commission*). The alternative, the use of *"only,"* is discussed in chapter 7, section A 5. If the passive voice is appropriate, use *"must"* rather than *"shall"* to indicate the imperative (*a report must include*, not *a report shall include*). The passive is appropriate only if there can be no doubt as to the actor.

5. Use *"May"* to Grant Discretion or Authority to Act

In chapter 7, section A 4, the use of *"shall"* is limited to imposing a duty to act. The corollary to this rule is that the use of *"may"* is limited to the grant of discretion or authority (*an aggrieved party may appeal a final judgment* or *the governor may fill a vacancy*). If a limitation is imposed on the exercise of the discretion or authority, introduce the limitation by the term *"only"* (*an aggrieved party may appeal a final judgment only by filing a notice of appeal within 30 days of the entry of judgment* or *the governor may fill a vacancy only from a list of three persons nominated by the commission*) (See the last paragraph in chapter 7, section A 4 for an alternative to this technique.)

Some writers on legal drafting suggest that the phrase *"in its discretion"* may be added to *"may"* to emphasize the intent to grant discretion.[4] This is bad advice. In addition to adding words and being redundant, the use of *"in its discretion"* on some occasions and not on others may lead a court to conclude that more discretion is intended to be granted by the phrase *"may in its discretion"* than by the simple *"may."* Discretion is discretion. The only limitations imposed on it are by the express terms of the legislation or rule, and not implied by the use of the redundant *"in its discretion."* Do not use it.

Another common use of *"may"* is to express eligibility or entitlement (*a classified employee with 30 years of service may retire at age 55* or *a committee member may be reimbursed for actual and necessary expenses while on committee business*). The use of *"may"* in these circumstances is unclear in that the provision could be read to establish the discretion in someone else such as an employer or administrator. To avoid this lack of clarity, the drafter should not use *"may"* but should state the eligibility or entitlement expressly in those terms (*a classified employee with 30 years of service is eligible to retire at age 55* or *a committee member is entitled to be reimbursed for actual and necessary expenses while on committee business*).

6.   Use *"May Not"* to Prohibit an Action

When a legal drafter wishes to prohibit an action, the most common method is to combine the mandatory *"shall"* with the negative *"not"* and say the actor *"shall not . . ."* (*a person shall not discharge a toxic substance into the air*). This form is incorrect. As is pointed out in chapter 6, section F, technically the words *"shall not"* only means that a person does not have a duty to engage in the action. The use of *"no person shall"* is just as incorrect because the phrase means only that there is no one who has a duty to engage in the action.

The proper way to express a prohibition to act is to say *"may not"* in connection with the action prohibited (*a person may not discharge a toxic substance into the air*). The effect of the words *"may not"* is to deny the actor the power or the authority to engage in the action. The denial of the power or authority accomplishes all that is necessary to establish the legal prohibition against a person performing an act. It also provides the legal basis for imposing a sanction for a violation of the prohibition. Nothing else is necessary.

7.   Use the Positive Rather than the Negative

When drafting a provision, it is often possible to express it in the positive (*a person is eligible* or *the administrator shall grant*) or in the negative (*a person is not ineligible* or *the administrator may not deny*). Dickerson refers to the use of the positive rather than the negative as *"directness."*[5] Wydick points out that the use of the negative when the positive can be used usually involves the use of multiple negatives (*not ineligible, not deny*).[6]

When possible, legal drafter should use the positive rather than the negative. The multiple negative is more difficult to understand and uses more words. The use of the negative *"not"* is an obvious indicator of a negative. A multiple negative arises when *"not"* is used with a word that also is a negative. The latter include words that begin with a negative prefix (*in-, un-,* or *non-*) or have a negative effect (*deny, refuse, prohibit, reject*).

Just because a word begins with what may be a negative prefix does not mean the word is a negative. A statute that reads *"a person may not operate a motor vehicle while intoxicated"* is not to be rejected in favor of *"a person may operate a motor vehicle only while sober." "Intoxicated"* may be the opposite of *"sober,"* but it is not a negative, at least in a grammatical sense.

8.   Use Tabulation for Multiple Actions

The rules governing tabulation are set out in chapter 8, section G. They apply to multiple actions as well as to multiple actors.

B.   THE OBJECT OF THE VERB OR THE COMPLEMENT OF THE ACTOR

As noted in chapter 5, a sentence is divided into a subject and a predicate. Chapter 6 discusses the actor as the subject of the sentence. The predicate is composed of a verb and an object or complement. The action as the verb is discussed in chapter 7 section A. The second part of the predicate is a verb completion, called either an object or a complement. When the verb in the sentence is a transitive verb, an object is required to complete the thought. An object can be either a person or a thing. In the sentence *"the commission shall appoint a director"* the *"director"* is the object of the verb *"appoint."* In the sentence *"a party may file a motion"* the *"motion"* is the object of the verb *"file."* A verb can also be intransitive, that is one that does not show action but rather links the subject to a noun, adjective, or clause called a complement. In the sentence *"a person is eligible to receive benefits at age 55"* the verb is *"is"* and the phrase *"eligible to receive benefits at age 55"* is the complement to *"person."* In legal drafting the intransitive verbs are most often used to declare status or in definitions.

The principles discussed in chapter 6 that apply to the actor also apply to the object or the complement. The only additional rule is that there must be agreement between the actor and its complement as to number (singular or plural).

Two principles applicable to the actor that may cause lack of clarity if applied to an object—those on the use of the singular and the articles *"a"* or *"an,"* discussed in chapter 6, sections A and C. Under those rules, a provision that reads *"the administrator may appoint an assistant administrator"* would mean that the administrator could appoint not just one assistant administrator but as many as the administrator desired. If the intent is to authorize the appointment of only one assistant, the provision should specify *"one assistant administrator."* If, however, the intent is to permit the appointment of one or more assistants, then the provision should say *"one or more assistant administrators"* or *"the number of assistant administrators as determined by the administrator."* The first alternative is preferable because it uses fewer words. Tabulation as discussed in chapter 8, section G is often important because there will often be multiple objects or complements.

Endnotes

1. R. Dickerson, The Fundamentals of Legal Drafting 3 (2d ed. 1986).
2. Id.
3. R. Wydick, Plain English For Lawyers 33 (4th ed. 1998).
4. R. Dickerson, supra note 1 at 214.
5. Id. at 184.
6. R. Wydick, supra note 3 at 75–76.

Chapter 8

GENERAL RULES

A. USE ONLY NECESSARY WORDS

1. Introduction

One of the premises of the Plain English movement is that the elimination of unnecessary words enhances the readability and understanding of what is written.[1] This principle (stated positively in the title of this section to comply with another Plain English principle) is important in all legal drafting. While many private legal documents such as letters, memoranda, briefs, and contracts are prepared for a small, known audience, and are effective for a short time only, there are also many such as adhesion contracts, pension plans, labor agreements, deed restrictions, organization bylaws, and corporate governance and financial provisions that affect thousands of persons beyond those who negotiate, draft, and sign or adopt them. Further, a contract is often designed to reflect the intent of those who voluntarily negotiate and become parties to it and is subject to interpretation by primarily those parties (and a court if litigation results). Many other documents, legislation, and rules, on the other hand, affect many people, most of whom are not known in advance. They are effective for an unlimited time, are designed to reflect the intent of a group of persons who may never see it in its final form and who themselves may not be affected by them. They govern the conduct of and are interpreted by others who had no role in their drafting. Further, when called upon to construe the documents, legislation or rules, courts follow canons of construction they presume the signatories or adopting bodies had in mind when they acted. They do this without any evidence that the signatories or members of the bodies were familiar with the canons of construction or gave them any thought in the drafting process.

One canon of construction has special relevance to the Use Only Necessary Words principle: the rule that courts will endeavor to give effect to every word of a document, legislation, or rule. The presumption of the canon is that those who signed or adopted the document, legislation, or rule chose each word with care and would not have included a word unless it intended the word to have some effect. The court will make every effort not to treat a word in a document, legislation or rule as mere surplusage. This being the case, the directive to eliminate unnecessary words rises from a mere principle of good writing to an imperative in legal drafting. Each word in a document, legislation, or rule adds or subtracts from the meaning of other words used. Each word invites those who must interpret the document, legislation, or rule, particularly courts, to engage in statutory construction to find a specific intent behind the word when, if the word is truly surplus, none exists.

2. Identify Working Words and Glue Words

Two of the most helpful techniques in eliminating unnecessary words are to focus on the who and the what, as explained in chapter 6, and to use the active voice, as explained in chapter 7, section A. Another is Wydick's suggestion to distinguish between two types of words in a sentence—working words that carry the meaning or substance of the sentence, and glue words that join the working words to make a sentence.[2] The working words are the nouns, verbs, adverbs, and adjectives, and the glue words are articles and prepositions.

Consider the following statutory provision:

All challenges for cause or favor, whether to the array or panel or to individual jurors, shall be determined by the court (28 U.S.C.A § 1870).

This sentence has 22 words. The working words are "all," "challenges," "cause," "favor," "array," "panel," "individual," "jurors," "determined," and "court," a total of ten words. The remaining 12 words are glue words. Convert this sentence to the active voice and put the words in the singular and the sentence reads:

"The court shall determine a challenge for cause or favor to an array, panel, or individual juror."

This sentence has 17 words. It has only 9 working words, and the glue words have been reduced from 12 to 8. The drafter could also eliminate one additional working word—"individual." To say that a party can challenge a juror is the same as saying that a party can challenge an individual juror. The word individual adds nothing except to make those reading the statute wonder, if only briefly, if there is any kind of juror other than an individual juror.

3. Avoid Compound Constructions or Expressions

Virtually every author on good writing style or legal or legislative drafting has preached the virtue of using short words or expressions rather than longer and more complicated ones or eliminating the word or expression. (Note—A common tendency would be to add the word *"altogether"* at the end of the preceding sentence. It would, of course, add nothing to the word "eliminate," which is an absolute.)

Strunk and White put the expressions *"the fact that," "who is," "which was," "in some (many) cases," "of a _____ character," "of a _____ nature"* among those that should not be used because they add nothing to the words that follow them.[3] Other compound constructions or expressions with their simpler alternatives as suggested by Dickerson, Flesch, and Wydick that are most relevant to a drafter of legislation or a rule include the following:[4]

compound	simple
a person is prohibited from	*a person may not*
adequate number of	*enough*
all of the	*all the*
at such time as	*when*
at that point (in time)	*then*
at the time	*when*
by means of	*by*
by reason of	*because of*
by virtue of	*by, under*
cause it to be done	*have it done*
does not operate to	*does not*
during such time as	*while*
during the course of	*during*
enter into an agreement with	*to agree with*
excessive number of	*too many*
for the duration of	*during*
for the purpose of	*to*
for the reason that	*because*
inasmuch as	*since*
in a case in which	*when (not where)*
in a prompt (or similar word) manner	*promptly*
in accordance with	*by, under*
in connection with	*with, about, concerning*
in favor of	*for*
in order to	*to*
in relation to	*about, concerning*
in the case of	*if*
in the event that	*if*
in the event of	*if*
in the nature of	*like*
is a person who	*a person*
is able to	*can*
is applicable to	*applies*
is authorized to	*may*
is binding upon	*binds*
is directed to	*shall*
is empowered (entitled)	*may*
is not prohibited from	*may*
is permitted to	*may*
is required to	*shall*
is unable to	*cannot*

compound	**simple**
it is directed	*shall*
it is lawful to	*may*
it is the duty of	*shall*
it is unlawful to	*may not*
or, in the alternative	*or*
paragraph 8 of subsection (c) of section 1984	*section 1984(c)(8)*
period of time	*period (time)*
prior to	*before*
provision of law	*provision*
subsequent to	*after*
sufficient number of	*enough*
the manner in which	*how*
the question as to whether	*whether*
to the effect that	*to*
under the provisions of	*under*
until such time as	*until*
used for _____ purposes	*used for _____*
with a view to	*to*
whenever	*when*
with reference to	*about, concerning*
with the object of achieving (or other gerund)	*to achieve (or other infinitive)*

4. Avoid Redundant Legal Phrases

Another technique to eliminate unnecessary words in legal drafting is to avoid traditional legal phrases that include redundancies. Although history explains how these redundant phrases crept into legal documents, it does not justify their continued use in a document, legislation, or a rule. The law does not require their use and they simply create problems for the reader of a document, legislation, or rule.[5] More importantly, they force a court to choose between ignoring a word in the document, legislation, or rule or giving different meanings to two or more words that were intended to be synonyms or were used without thought.

Some common legally redundant expressions are:

> *advise and consent*
> *alter or amend*
> *cease and desist*
> *confess and acknowledge*
> *for and during the period*
> *force and effect*
> *free and clear*
> *full and complete*
> *give, devise, and bequeath*
> *good and sufficient*
> *last will and testament*
> *make and enter into*

null and void
order and direct
perform and discharge
save and except
to have and to hold
transfer and assign
true and correct
undertake and agree
unless and until

The use of two words joined by an *"and"* is a red flag that should make drafters pause and examine carefully whether both words are necessary or whether one is redundant and should be eliminated.

Some compound constructions are worse than redundancies; they include inconsistent terms. The expression *"authorize and direct"* includes a word that grants discretion, *"authorize,"* and one that is mandatory, *"direct."* Similar expressions are *"means and includes"* and *"desire and require."* Use the word that most accurately reflects the intent, and leave out the other. Other constructions use two words, one of which includes the other such as *"from and after," "have and hold,"* and *"by and between."* Again, use the most accurate and leave out the other.

B. USE COMMON WORDS

Another premise of the Plain English movement is the basic truth that words in common, every day usage by persons of average intelligence and education are more easily read and understood than words that require a high level of education or specialized knowledge.[6]

In no area of legal writing is this principle more important than in drafting documents, legislation, and rules. As explained at the beginning of this chapter, most other types of legal drafting are intended for a known and usually limited audience and have a limited duration. Legislation, rules, and some types of private documents, however, usually have vast and unknown audiences, in part because they usually are of unlimited duration, remaining in effect until a formal act of cancellation or repeal.

Not knowing the audience, the drafter of a general document, legislation, or rule has a special responsibility to use language that is easily understood by persons without a high level of education or specialized training. At what level of reader should legislation and rules be aimed? Suggestions have been made by both Flesch and Dickerson, with which we disagree. Flesch suggests at the 50 percent of the people who are below average in education, IQ, reading skill, or business experience.[7] Dickerson, on the other hand, suggests that the language of a statute or rule may vary depending upon the audience. In his view, a statute addressed to a highly specialized segment of the public such as government officials or the tobacco industry can be drafted differently from one addressed to the general public.[8]

To follow Flesch limits the drafter to language and concepts understandable by a child in grammar school. It should be noted that Flesch was concerned primarily with rules of the Federal Trade Commission that were designed to protect consumers, particularly those consumers who by reason of lack of education, basic intelligence, or ordinary experience, are unable to protect themselves in the market place. Perhaps an agency should draft a rule designed primarily to benefit an underprivileged class so a member of the class can understand it. Most documents, legislation, and rules should not be cast at that level, however, although simpler is usually better.

Even more objectionable is Dickerson's suggestion that a document, legislation, or rule designed to affect a particular group such as investors, homeowners, government officials, or tobacco companies may be drafted as though only they are concerned with its content. This view ignores two important facts about the audiences of documents, legislation, and rules. First, for every group directly affected there is a far larger group of intended persons who benefit or are burdened that have just as great an interest in the document, legislation, or rule. Organizational or government officials are not the only, or even the primary, group interested in the content and language of the document, legislation, or rule covering the officials. Persons affected by the actions of the officials may be even more concerned with the proper interpretation of the document, legislation, or rule than the officials themselves. Even persons not directly affected by the officials but who are merely concerned with the proper functioning of the organization or government are concerned with the language of the document, legislation or rule regulating officials. A document, legislation, or rule on conflict of interest is an obvious example. Second, these other persons are usually ordinary citizens who have a wide variety of backgrounds and education and are not likely to have any special qualification to interpret a document, legislation or a rule. The document, legislation or rule must, consequently, be drafted so as to be read and understood by the larger, less sophisticated group, not just the small group directly subject to the regulation. The same analysis applies to legislation or rules governing mutual funds. These regulations are just as important to investors and those affected by the stock market—virtually everyone. To argue that legislation or a rule regulating mutual funds can be drafted using language understandable only by persons in the industry is to miss the essential nature of legislation and rules. The reality as to any general document, legislation, or rule is that the drafter has no idea who its audience will be. Under these circumstances, the drafter must use language that can be understood by the general population and not some special segment of it. The only exception is the document that applies only to those who participated in its drafting and who are parties to it.

At what level should the drafter aim, if not the below average person or the specialized group? The question, framed in this way, essentially answers itself. Because of its unknown but possibly broad audience a general document, legislation, or rule should be drafted so it can be readily understood by a person of average intelligence, education, and experience. What is average? Without attempting to answer this question based on census or other data that might gives specifics (e.g., an I.Q. of 100, 10.3 years of education, and having purchased or leased a house and an automobile), the drafter should be able to assume a person who has successfully completed high school and can function adequately as an employee and consumer. The best comparison is probably a well written newspaper.

A long list of common words and their less common synonyms (e.g., *explain* and *elucidate* or *end* and *terminate*) is not given here because for almost every word in common usage there is a synonym that is less common and usually used only to convey formality or pretentiousness. The principle is simple—use the common, avoid the uncommon.

C. AVOID LAWYERISMS (LEGALESE)

A corollary to the principle to use common words is to avoid the use of what good writing advocates call *"lawyerisms"* or *"legalese."* Lawyerisms are words or phrases used characteristically by lawyers or people trying to sound like lawyers. They are the jargon of the legal profession. They have been the curse of legal writing as long as there have been lawyers. Examples are *"said," "such," "whereas," "further provided that," "herein above mentioned," "appurtenances," "party of the first part," "the same," "therefore," "thereafter," "hereby," "hereinafter."* Lawyers are particularly addicted to the prefixes of *"here"* and *"there."* These words are almost never necessary and add nothing to substance. A drafter who discovers one of these words in a draft of document, legislation, or rule should make every effort to eliminate it or find a less artificial substitute. The drafter will usually discover that *"the"* or *"that"* will serve just as well as *"such"* or *"said"* or their variations.

Legal jargon can also creep into legislation or a rule in the form of a Latin or law French expression such as *"per curiam," "certiorari," "res judicata," "res ipsa loquitur," "res gestae," "sub curia," "caveat emptor," "a mensa et thoro,"* and *"a vincula matrimoni."* The legal drafter should not use these and similar phrases unless the purpose is to abolish or amend the legal rule behind the expression. When this occurs, the phrase should be defined to avoid any confusion as to just what legal rule is being changed.

D. BE CONSISTENT

Another traditional principle of good legal writing is to be consistent in the use of words. Consistency in this context means being repetitive, that is using the same word rather than a synonym. In non legal writing, the use of a synonym rather than being repetitive, known as "elegant variation," is considered desirable, but only as a matter of style. In legal writing elegant variation is undesirable because of the construction problems it may create.

In the drafting of a document, legislation, or rule, consistency in the use of language is an absolute necessity. Courts take the position that if the document, legislation, or rule uses one word one place and a slightly different word in another place, the document, legislation, or rule means something different in the latter than in the former. In the world of construction, there is no elegant variation, only substantive variation. The courts will conclude only reluctantly that no difference in substance was intended. Wydick refers to elegant variation as a language quirk.[9] Its use in drafting legislation and rules is far worse. The legal drafter must be consistent in the use of words and avoid the trap of elegant variation and choose the best word the first and every time it is used.

The following are examples of synonyms that the unwary drafter may use.

attorney	- *lawyer, counsel*
author	- *writer*
automobile	- *car, vehicle*
case	- *action, suit, proceeding*
clothing	- *apparel*
decide	- *determine, rule*
file	- *submit*
house	- *home*
judge	- *judicial officer*
person	- *individual*
publisher	- *printer*
radio	- *receiver*
refine	- *purify*
reside	- *live*
road	- *street, roadway*
rule	- *regulation*
ship	- *boat, vessel*

Obviously, the list is endless. Because it is endless, the opportunities for the drafter to be inconsistent and thereby cause statutory construction problems are also endless.

E.   USE SHORT SENTENCES

Of all of the complaints made about legal drafting, probably the most common and the most justified is that sentences in them are too long. This is particularly true of the federal Internal Revenue Code. Every lawyer or critic of legal drafting has a favorite example of the sentence in a document, legislation, or rule that runs on for hundreds of words and includes five or ten separate thoughts. The entire passage, and each separate thought, could be far more easily understood if the sentence were broken down into a separate sentence for each separate thought.

Long sentences are common in documents, legislation, and rules in part because their use by lawyers in all types of legal writing is traditional. Two additional factors are particularly applicable to legal drafting. One is the fear of the drafter that, if all parts of a provision are not in the same sentence, a court construing the provision might not realize the relationship between the parts and might construe one sentence without regard to its companion sentences. This is particularly true as to a qualifier or proviso.

The second reason lies in the drafting process itself. Although a sentence in a document, legislation, or rule may start out as a single thought simply expressed, as the sentence is reviewed by other persons, groups, and committees, additional ideas are added by subsidiary clauses added to the original sentence, with or without punctuation marks such as commas or semicolons. Proponents of a subsidiary clause are more interested in incorporating their pet idea into the document, legislation, or rule than with the length or readability of the entire sentence. They are satisfied if they see the language they want in the sentence. The original drafter may not have responsibility for adding the new language or, if still involved, may be primarily concerned with accommodating the proponents of the additional language and not in following principles of good drafting. In either case, the document, legislation, or rule becomes the product of a committee of drafters rather than one individual, with all of the unfortunate characteristics of a committee product.

When the original drafter loses responsibility for incorporating additional ideas into the original draft, little can be done to prevent total loss of adherence to the short sentence principle. If, however, the original drafter is responsible for revising the original draft to reflect the additions, the drafter should not abandon good drafting, including short sentences. The task may be more difficult, but for that very reason it is important. If simple expression is too much for the drafter, the likelihood that those to whom the legislation or rule applies or who must administer it will not understand it and the courts are likely not to construe it correctly.

How then to keep sentences short? The key is to limit each sentence to a single idea or thought. If the idea or thought is subject to a qualifier such as to person, time, place, that is longer than a short phrase, put it in a separate sentence. If the sentence describes a series of events, put each event in a separate sentence. See the example of 28 U.S.C.A. § 2003 and its rewrite into shorter sentences given in chapter 7, section F.

In some types of legal writing, such as that which is merely descriptive or involves advocacy, the use of short sentences may result in objectionable choppiness. This is less of a problem in legal drafting because it primarily gives commands or states conditions. Choppiness in this type of writing is seldom a disadvantage but rather is to be preferred because it will aid understanding.

F. ARRANGE WORDS CAREFULLY

In chapter 6 the drafter was instructed to concentrate on the actor, action, and object or complement that is the subject, verb, and object or complement of a sentence. A major weakness of legal writing in general and of legal drafting in particular is to put qualifying language between the actor and the action or the action and the object or complement. This weakness separates the working words of the sentence, making it difficult for the reader to see the relationship between the actor, the action, and the object or complement. For example, 28 U.S.C.A § 2003 provides:

> *Whenever any such contingency arises after a marshal has sold any realty or interest therein and before a deed is executed, the court may, on application by the purchaser, or the plaintiff in whose action the sale was made, setting forth the facts of the case and the reason why the title was not perfected by such marshal, order the succeeding marshal to perfect the title and execute a deed to the purchaser, upon payment of the purchase money and unpaid costs.*

The actor in this provision is the court, the action is to order, and the object is the succeeding marshal's execution of a deed. There are four conditions on the issuance of the order: (1) the contingency expressed in the previous paragraph (seizure of property by a marshal no longer in office); (2) the previous marshal selling the property and then (3) leaving office before executing a deed; and (4) an application by a purchaser or plaintiff in the action in which the property was sold reciting the facts of the case and the reason why the previous marshal did not convey title. A fifth condition is on the execution of a deed—the purchaser must pay the purchase price and unpaid costs. The first three conditions on the order are properly located at the beginning of the sentence and the condition on the execution of the deed is properly at the sentence's end. The sentence is made much more difficult to understand, however, by the insertion of the fourth condition, a total of 34 words, between the actor (the court) and the action (the order). Expressing all four conditions together prior to reference to the court is preferable because it would permit the actor, action, and object to be placed together. With this change, and following other principles expressed elsewhere in this book, the provision would read:

> *If this contingency arises after a marshal has sold realty or interest in realty but before a deed is executed, the purchaser or plaintiff in the action in which the sale was made may file an application explaining why the deed was not executed. On the application, the court may order the successor marshal to execute a deed to the purchaser. The marshal shall execute the deed upon payment of the purchase money and unpaid costs.*

The revision has several advantages over the original. First, the condition of filing the application is moved from between the actor and the action—the court and the order—and put in its proper place chronologically, after the seizure of realty by a marshal, sale of the realty by the marshal, and the marshal leaving office before executing a deed. Second, it divides the one long sentence of 82 words into three shorter sentences. Third, the number of words is reduced from 82 to 76. Further reduction could probably be made by referring only to realty and not also to interests in realty. Fourth, it is made clear that the fifth condition—payment by the purchaser—is a condition only to execution of the deed by the new marshal and not to the application and the court order, an interpretation that is possible under the original version. Fifth, the lack of consistency between references to executing a deed and perfecting title is eliminated.

The revision also clarifies the restriction that a court order can be made only on the application and not by the court on its own motion. In the drafting process, a drafter should inquire whether the proponent of the provision really wants to require an application before the court can order the marshal to convey the property to the purchaser. An even more basic question is then raised—why is it necessary to have a special provision on the power of the successor marshal to execute a deed for property seized and sold by a predecessor in office?

In 28 U.S.C.A. § 2003 quoted above, the separation was between the actor and the action. The separation can also be between the action and the object. That section would include the latter defect if the clause read *"the court may order, on application by the purchaser . . . , the succeeding marshal to perfect the title. . . ."* The latter separation is just as much to be avoided as the former because it creates the same problem for the reader.

The proper placement of the word *"only"* often creates difficulties for the drafter. If *"only"* is placed inappropriately, a provision may have an effect quite different from that intended by the drafter.

Here are some possibilities:

Only the governor may appoint a person nominated by the commission.

The governor only may appoint a person nominated by the commission.

The governor may only appoint a person nominated by the commission.

The governor may appoint only a person nominated by the commission.

The governor may appoint a person only nominated by the commission.

The governor may appoint a person nominated by the commission only.

To say *"The governor only may appoint a person nominated by the commission"* is confusing because it is not clear whether *"only"* modifies *"governor," "appoint,"* or *"person."* While a person reading the provision will probably figure out that the purpose of the provision is not to limit the appointing power to the governor or what the governor may do with a nominee, but is intended to restrict the governor's appointing power to persons nominated by the commission, the drafter can eliminate the confusion by drafting the provision to read *"The governor may appoint only a person nominated by the commission."*

The basic rule to follow is the same as to each type of modifier, whether adjective, adverb, or an entire clause—place it as close as possible to the word or words it modifies. This will avoid or at least reduce the chance that the modifier will be applied to the wrong word.

G. TABULATE TO SIMPLIFY

One of the best techniques for the drafter to eliminate unnecessary words and to enhance clarity is to tabulate multiples of the actor, action, object, complement, or qualifiers of any of them. The use of tabulation in the drafting process has another important benefit—to aid the drafter and the proponent in identifying all of the variables, including only those intended for inclusion and excluding the others.

An example of a rule whose clarity would be enhanced by tabulation is Ohio Rule of Civil Procedure 4(B) concerning the summons to be issued by a clerk of court upon the filing of a complaint. The first sentence of the rule reads:

> *The summons shall be signed by the clerk, contain the name and address of the court and the names and addresses of the parties, be directed to the defendant, state the name and address of the plaintiff's attorney, if any, otherwise the plaintiff's address, and the times within which these rules or any statutory provision require the defendant to appear and defend and shall notify him that in case of his failure to do so, judgment by default will be rendered against him for the relief demanded in the complaint.*

The rule contains three separate directions to the clerk: (1) direct the summons to the defendant; (2) include certain information in the summons; and (3) sign the summons. The information to be included is of three types, names, addresses, and notices. The names and addresses are of four classes—the court, plaintiff, defendant, and the plaintiff's attorney. Notice of two facts must also be included, when the defendant must appear and defend and what will happen if the defendant fails to defend. In the rule all of these items are included in a single sentence of 90 words, with eight commas as the only punctuation.

Tabulating everything in the rule, and using the other drafting principles in the book, the rule would read:

> *The clerk shall:*
>
> *(1) direct the summons to the defendant;*
>
> *(2) include in the summons:*
>
>   *(A) the name and address of the*

       (i) court,

       (ii) plaintiff,

       (iii) defendant, and

       (iv) plaintiff's attorney; and

    (B) notice

       (i) of the time specified by statute or rule in which the defendant must appear and defend, and

       (ii) that if the defendant fails to appear and depend, a default judgment will be rendered for the relief requested in the complaint; and

(3) sign the summons.

The revised rule has a number of advantages over the original. It is shorter, 70 words rather than 90. It is in the active voice. Each of the three actions to be taken by the clerk—direct, include, and sign—is put next to the object of the verb. It lists the actions in the order in which the words will appear in the summons—first the direction, second the necessary information, and third the signature of the clerk. In addition, it eliminates the masculine references in the old rule.

The revised rule is broken down so that each multiple is tabulated. This results in three levels of tabulation, which for the sake of readability may be too many. It may be preferable not to tabulate the three duties of the clerk—direct, include, and sign—but to put the direct and sign duties first, and to tabulate only the information to be included in the summons. The rule would then read:

The clerk shall direct the summons to the defendant, sign it, and include in it:

(1) the name and address of the

    (A) court,

    (B) plaintiff,

    (C) defendant, and

    (D) plaintiff's attorney; and

(2) notice

    (A) of the time specified by rule or statute in which the defendant must appear and defend, and

    (B) that if the defendant fails to appear and defend, a default judgment will be rendered for the relief requested in the complaint.

Several guidelines are useful in determining when to tabulate in the initial draft:

    1.   The repetition of a noun or verb, particularly a command (*shall*) or authorization (*may*) in a section, paragraph, or sentence is a very good indicator that tabulation may be appropriate. Similar-

ly the use of *"and"* or *"or"* indicates a series that calls for tabulation. Within a sentence, if there are only two items in the series and each item includes only a few words, tabulation is not necessary (*a witness shall swear or affirm before testifying*). If each item contains a substantial number of words, the use of letters or numbers to set off each item, but without tabulating them, may be the most helpful (*within 30 days of acceptance, an applicant shall indicate its intention to (1) enroll in the class to begin the following September or (2) defer admission for a period of up to two years*).

As helpful as tabulation can be, it can also be overdone. Flesch has pointed out that Dickerson, who has contributed so much to the improvement in legal and legislative drafting, has gone too far in advocating the virtues of tabulation. According to Flesch, Dickerson accepted Layman Allen's symbolic logic approach to legal drafting that utilized "systematic pulverization." Dickerson converted this into his tabulation style of legal drafting. Flesch calls excessive tabulation "shredded English."[10] Because short and complete sentences almost disappear in an effort to avoid ambiguity by isolating each element of a provision in a document, legislation, or rule, they are replaced by a tabulation that can run on for pages. A computer programmed for symbolic language may be able to track the meaning of the provision, but an ordinary mortal who has only a printed copy of the legislation or rule is left totally confused. A tabulation should not be used when it does not help readability and understanding. It should rarely be used in a definition that is merely a listing of the types of things included in the word defined. It should also rarely be used to string together a whole series of provisions that can stand as separate sentences. Excessive tabulation is one of the primary reasons why so many federal statutes and rules defy comprehension.

2.   The placement of a time limitation or other qualifier on a series can often create problems in a document, legislation, or rule. If placed at the end of the series, it is not always clear whether the qualifier applies only to the last of the series or to each. In the example in the preceding paragraph, the qualifier *"within 30 days of acceptance"* is placed at the beginning of the sentence to make it clear that it applied to both enrollment in the next class and deferral to a later class. If it were placed at the end of the sentence, it could be interpreted to mean that only a notice of deferral had to be given within the 30 day limit. Or placed between *"shall"* and *"indicate"* (*an applicant shall, within 30 days of acceptance, indicate . . .*) it would be incorrect because it would separate the actor and the action, as discussed in chapter 9, section F.

3.   In a tabulation, an *"and"* or an *"or"* will usually precede the last item in the series.[11] A total of four *ands* are used in the

tabulation given at the beginning of this subsection of Ohio Rule of Civil Procedure 4(B) concerning the summons issued by the clerk of court. The first *"and"* is after *"defendant"* in (2)(A)(iii) to indicate that the names and addresses of all four classes listed in (i)-(iv) are required. Another *"and"* is after *"plaintiff's attorney"* in (2)(A)(iv) to join the two types of information that must be included in the summons specified in (A) and (B). A third *"and"* is at the end of 2(B)(i) to show that the notice requirement is twofold. The fourth *"and"* is at the end of (2)(B)(ii) to show that (1), (2), and (3) are all obligations of the clerk.

The *"and,"* of course, makes all the obligations in the rule cumulative. If a listing in the tabulation is meant to be in the alternative rather than cumulative, then *"or"* rather than *"and"* will be used. (*A corporation may be sued in any judicial district in which it is incorporated or licensed to do business or is doing business . . . .*) *(28 U.S.C.A. § 139(c))*.

Problems are created when the listing is neither cumulative in the sense that all must be included, nor in the alternative in the sense that only one of the list may be required or chosen. The following provision is an example:

A violation of this section is punishable by:

   (1) a fine of $10,000,

   (2) imprisonment for six months,

   (3) suspension of driving privileges for one year, (and) (or)

   (4) participation in an alcohol abuse program.

In this statute *"and"* would be appropriate only if the court is required to impose all of the penalties. On the other hand *"or"* would be appropriate only if each of the four penalties were exclusive, that is, one and only one of them could be imposed. If the intent of the drafter is to authorize the court to impose any combination of the penalties, do not use either *"and"* or *"or"* at the end of clause (3), but add the words *"one or more of the following"* just before the tabulation. The introductory clause would then read *"a violation of this section is punishable by one or more of the following . . . . "*

4. In a tabulation, the first word of each item tabulated must be of the same class and be appropriate to the introductory or succeeding phrase. Again using the example of Ohio Rule of Civil Procedure 4(B) discussed at the beginning of this subsection, each of the items tabulated begins with a verb, *"direct,"* *"include,"* and *"sign,"* and is a duty of the clerk. It would not be appropriate to add a fourth item such as *"may include any other information requested by the plaintiff"* or *"other information requested by the plaintiff"* because neither would be appropriate to follow the *"shall"* in the introductory phrase. The language

"other information requested by the plaintiff" would be appropriately added to subsection (2)(A) as clause (v), but the clause *"may include any other information requested by the plaintiff"* would not because the *"may include"* does not fit with the *"shall"* in the introductory clause.

H. PUNCTUATE PROPERLY

An early rule of statutory construction held that punctuation is not part of a statute. Today a legal drafter would be ill advised to ignore punctuation. The reasons for this principle are simple. Those who sign or adopt a document, legislation or rule do so with punctuation marks in it. As a consequence, courts look at punctuation marks in legislation or a rule in the same way that they look at its words—as guides to legislative intent. A court can disregard a punctuation mark for the same reason it can disregard a word—if the court considers doing so necessary to discover and implement the signers' or adopters' intent.

The basic rules of punctuation will not be reviewed here. They can be easily obtained in any book on basic grammar such as the recent and surprisingly popular book Eats, Shoots and Leaves by Lynne Truss. There are, however, several uses of punctuation marks that often create problems for the drafter or reader of legislation or a rule. To avoid these problems, follow these principles:

1. Always put a comma before the *"and"* or *"or"* in a series when the last two words in the series are intended to be separate (*a brief must contain a statement of issues, statement of the case, statement of facts, argument, and conclusion*).[12] In this example, the comma before the *and* is necessary to show that the argument and conclusion are each a separate part of the brief. If there were no comma, it would be possible to read the words *"argument and conclusion"* to mean that the last section of the brief would include both an argument and a conclusion. The comma before the *"and"* eliminates the possibility of confusion and misinterpretation.

2. Use a comma to indicate that qualifying language is applicable to all of the preceding clauses (*the court may receive additional evidence in writing or by oral testimony, unless the court decides it is merely cumulative*). Here without the comma after testimony it would not be clear whether the *"unless"* clause applies to both written evidence and oral testimony or only to the latter. In many instances, placing the qualifying language first is preferable.

3. If a comma is necessary to separate the clauses of a compound sentence joined by an *"and"* or other conjunction, make each clause a separate sentence. The sentence that reads

    Whenever a civil action is filed in a court and the court finds that there is a want of jurisdic-

> *tion, the court shall, if it is in the interests of justice, transfer such action to any other court in which the action could have been brought at the time it was filed and the action shall proceed as if it had been filed in the court to which transferred on the date upon which it was filed in the court from which it is transferred (abbreviated from 28 U.S.C.A. § 1631).*

should be divided into two sentences as follows:

> *Whenever a civil action is filed in a court and the court finds that there is a want of jurisdiction, the court shall, if it is in the interests of justice, transfer such action to any other court in which the action could have been brought at the time it was filed. The action shall proceed as if it had been filed in the court to which transferred on the date upon which it was filed in the court from which it is transferred.*

(Note that the only revision made here is to divide the separate clauses into two sentences. Many other revisions would be necessary to have the section conform to the other principles expressed in this book.)

4. Use semicolons only in tabulations. (See chapter 8, section G for a discussion of tabulation.) Do not use semicolons as a substitute for a period to separate independent clauses in a sentence.

   The provision that reads

   > *Issues not demanded for trial by jury as provided in Rule 38 shall be tried by the court; but, notwithstanding the failure of a part to demand a jury in an action in which such demand might have been made of right, the court in its discretion upon motion may order a trial by a jury of any or all issues. (Federal Rule of Civil Procedure 39(b)).*

   should read

   > *Issues not demanded for trial by jury as provided in Rule 38 shall be tried by the court. Notwithstanding the failure of a party to demand a jury trial in an action in which such demand might have been made of right, the court in it discretion upon motion may order a trial by a jury of any or all issues.*

(Again, the only revision made is to divide the sentence into two sentences.)

5. Use a colon only to introduce a tabulation. Do not use it to introduce a proviso. Make the proviso a separate sentence. (See chapter 8, section J 3 for a discussion of provisos.)

I. DEFINITIONS

One of the most useful tools of a legal drafter is the definition. A definition can assist the drafter in a number of ways. It avoids repetition and thereby reduces the number of words in a document, legislation, or rule. It avoids inconsistency by defining the word only once. It aids in precision by not leaving it up to the reader to define the word. It also permits the drafter to control what a word means, and not leave it up to a dictionary.

Definitions can be classified in a number of ways. "Real" and "nominal," "lexical" and "stipulative," or by method—synonym, analysis, synthesis, and denotative. These classifications are of little help to the drafter and will not be used here. For most drafting only 7 principles are important.

1. Use a definition only when the meaning of a word is important and it is used more than once in a chapter, part, section, subsection, or paragraph.

2. Include a definition of a word only in the subdivision of a document, legislation, or rule to which it is applicable. If the word defined is used throughout a chapter, the definition section of the chapter should begin with *"in this chapter _____ means (or includes)...."* If the word is used only in a subsection, the definition section of the subsection should begin with *"in this subsection _____ means (or includes)...."*

3. Put the definition at the beginning of the subdivision of the legislation or rule in which the word defined is used, i.e., at the beginning of a chapter if it is used in the entire chapter or at the beginning of a subsection or paragraph if it is used only in the subsection or the paragraph.

4. A definition should say that a word either *"means"* or *"includes"* the remainder of the words used in the definition. If the definition is intended to be exhaustive and exclude everything not included in the definition, use *"means."* If the definition is intended to be only partial and permit the word to be applied to things not included in the definition, use *"includes."* Do not say *"includes but is not limited to."* The words *"but is not limited to"* are redundant.

5. Do not define a word to mean something it is not usually understood to mean. Thus, do not define *"dog"* to include *"cat"* or *"solid"* to include *"liquid."* If a drafter finds that the word being defined does not normally include items included in the definition, use a different word. A drafter may use a word in a

specialized or technical meaning in a document, legislation, or a rule relating to a specialized area, but the word should be defined with reference to that activity.

6. Do not include a substantive provision in a definition. Do not say *"pleading means a complaint, answer, reply or motion, which must be served before filing."* The requirement as to service before filing should be put in a separate provision and included with the substantive provisions relating to service of pleadings and other documents.

7. Do not include the word defined in the definition. A definition that says that motor vehicle means *"a vehicle with a motor"* is not helpful. Inclusion of the word defined in the definition often occurs when a phrase of two or more words is used but only one requires a definition. If the phrase *"regional facility"* is used and the important word is regional, don't define it to mean *"a facility serving more than one state."* Instead define only *"regional"* to mean *"serving more than one state."* If the important word is facility, then define it. If each word is important, define each separately.

J. CONDITIONS, EXCEPTIONS, AND PROVISOS

1. Conditions

A condition is a statement of a prerequisite for the applicability of a provision. A condition is expressed by an *"if"* (*if the administrator finds an applicant has satisfied all of the conditions for eligibility, the administrator shall grant the application*). Do not use *"when"* or *"where"* to express a condition. A condition should be stated first unless there are several of them. If there are several, it is clearer to state the rule first and then the contingencies. If the conditions exceed two or are lengthy, they should be tabulated in accordance with chapter 8, section G.

"When" should be used only to express a time relationship between an event that it is assumed will occur and a subsequent event (*when the time for submitting an application has expired, the commission shall choose one of the applicants*, or *when the parties have completed their closing arguments, the judge shall instruct the jury*). *"Where"* should be used only to describe a spatial relationship (*the commission may not consider where the applicant resides*).

2. Exceptions

An exception is a statement of the circumstances under which the rule set out in a provision is not applicable. To introduce an exception, use the word *"except"* (*except as provided in Rule 9(e), an employee is entitled to the benefits provided by this chapter*) or state that the rule does not apply under specified circumstances (*this section does not apply if the spouse of the employee is covered by another qualified plan*). An exception should be included in an introductory phrase beginning with *"except"* and placed before the general rule as in the first example if the exception is not too long. A longer exception should be included in a separate sentence and stated after the general rule, as in the second example.

3. Provisos

A proviso is an exception or modification that begins with *"provided that"* or, if more than one proviso is added, *"provided further."* It follows the statement of the rule and is usually preceded by a comma or semicolon. A proviso should never be used. It is the lazy drafter's technique for adding qualifiers to a substantive provision. Its most common use is by legislators who add a qualifier to protect a special interest during floor debate or last minute negotiations or to amend an existing statute without rewriting the section being amended. Often one proviso after another is tacked on to a substantive provision so that the provisos often are far longer than the substantive provision. Even worse, additional substantive provisions are sometimes added as provisos even though they do not affect the original substantive provision. This is legal drafting at its worst but is usually beyond the control of the drafter.

K. PENALTY

One of the most difficult provisions for a legal drafter to prepare is the one that imposes a penalty. There are a number of ways to do this. It can be expressed in terms of: (1) the person who violates a provision (*a person who violates section 10* or *a person convicted of violating section 10*); (2) the violation itself (*a violation of section 10*); (3) the nature of the crime (*it is a felony to violate section 10*); (4) the penalty (*the penalty for violating section 10 is . . .*); or (5) the court (*a court that convicts a person of violating section 10 . . .*).

The clearest and most concise way to provide for the imposition of a penalty is to state it in terms of the penalty (*the penalty for violating section 10 is . . .*). This form uses the fewest words, conforms to principles of good drafting, and has as the subject of the sentence the principal reason for including the sentence in the document, legislation, or rule—the penalty.

In establishing the penalty, the drafter can provide for a simple or multiple penalties (*a fine* or *a fine and imprisonment*) and establish a maximum (*a fine not to exceed $500*), a minimum and a maximum (*a fine not less than $100 nor more than $500*) or fixed (*a sentence of 6 months*). If there are multiple penalties, the principles that govern tabulation as detailed in section 8 G are applicable. To avoid lack of clarity, the drafter should always use *"or"* rather than *"and"* before the last listed penalty (*a fine of $500 or a sentence of 6 months*) if each penalty is exclusive. If the penalties are not intended to be mutually exclusive the listing should be followed by *"or both"* if there are only two (*a fine of $500, a sentence of 6 months, or both*) or *"or a combination of them"* if more than two (*a* *fine of $100, a sentence of 6 months, community service of 500 hours, or a combination of them).*

It is not necessary or desirable to add the words *"in the discretion of the court"* to a penalty that is not mandatory because the establishment of a range of penalty necessarily means that the court must exercise discretion in imposing a particular penalty.

In some jurisdictions, the drafter need not establish the penalty directly but need only classify the crime as a certain type of felony or misdemeanor. In these jurisdictions a separate statute provides the penalty for each crime classification (*a felony third class is punishable by a fine not to exceed $10,000, a sentence of imprisonment not to exceed 10 years, or both*). The classification section in these jurisdictions should read *"a violation of section 10 is a felony third class."*

L. CREATION OF AN AGENCY, ENTITY, OR OFFICE

Often a document, legislation or a rule will create an entity or office to administer or carry out duties under it. Sometimes the document, legislation, or rule will merely state that the entity or officer shall do something without expressly providing for the creation of the entity or office. On other occasions, the document, legislation, or rule will place the authority in the entity or office in one provision and state what the authority is in another. A third alternative is to provide expressly for the creation of the entity or the office in one provision and to grant it authority in another. The first type of provision is all that is necessary. It should read *"the Department of Energy shall regulate the production of oil."* This type of provision both creates the entity and grants authority. Either of the other two alternatives takes two separate provisions to accomplish the same thing.

M. CROSS REFERENCES

A cross reference to another section of a bill, rule, or codification of legislation or rules can be a boon to the drafter but a bane to the reader. The virtue of a cross reference is that it saves words and ensures consistency. Its drawback is that all of the material necessary to understand the legislation or rule is not immediately before the reader. Cross references are helpful if used sparingly and if it is reasonable to assume that the material to which a cross reference is made is likely to be readily available to the reader.

In making a cross reference, do not refer to relative location (*the last paragraph, the immediately preceding section*). Instead, refer to the precise paragraph or section (*paragraph 6(b)(1)(A)* or *section 6*). Use parentheses if they are used in the cross referenced material. Do not spell out the sections, subsections, and paragraphs (*clause (A) of paragraph 1 of subsection (b) of section 6*). The example itself demonstrates why it should not be used.

A lack of clarity that can arise in a cross reference is whether the cross reference is to a document, legislation, or rule as it existed on the day of the adoption of the new document, legislation, or rule or at the time the new document, legislation, or rule is construed. This issue becomes important if the prior document, legislation, or rule has been amended in the interim. The general rule is that absent words to the contrary a cross reference is to specific prior document, legislation, or rule as it existed at the time of the adoption of the new document, legislation, or rule, not when the latter is construed.[13] Thus a subsequent amendment is not incorporated into the cross reference. If the contrary is intended, the cross reference should provide *"including an amendment subsequent to the enactment of this Act (or adoption of this rule)."* The latter type of provision can be subject to a challenge on the ground that it is an unlawful delegation of authority.

N. NUMBERS, DATES, TIME, AND AGE

1. Numbers

There are three types of numbers that a legal drafter may use: cardinal numbers (*1, 2, 3*), ordinal (*first, second*), and fractional (*one fifth, two thirds*). A cardinal number is expressed as a figure as indicated (*the court shall hear the case 7 days after the last brief is filed*). If the number begins the sentence, it is spelled out (*Seven days after the last brief is filed the court shall hear the case*). Ordinal and fractional numbers are spelled out as indicated.

2. Dates

Use a cardinal number rather than an ordinal number to express a date (*December 25* rather than *the twenty fifth day of December*). A common mistake is to convert *the twenty fifth day of December* to "*December 25th.*" This is incorrect. The ordinal "*twenty fifth*" is an adjective that modifies "*day*" and thus cannot stand alone. Set off the year by two commas when used with the month and day (*December 25, 1990,*) but use only the comma after the year when only the month is used (*in December 1990,*).

3. Time

In a document, legislation, or rule, time can mean the time of day or a period of time. When expressing the time of day, use cardinal numbers (*the applicant shall file an application before 5:00 p.m. on the last day of the month*). When expressing a period of time, the drafter must avoid ambiguity in when the period of time begins or ends. Do not use "*from*" a date to begin a period (*from January 1, 1991,*) or "*to,*" "*until,*" or "*by*" to end a period (*to (until, by) July 1, 1991,*). Instead use "*after*" with the immediately preceding date to start the running of time (*after December 31, 1990,*) and "*before*" with the immediately succeeding date to end the period (*before July 1, 1991,*).

4. Age

When expressing age, the drafter must remember that a person reaches an age on the person's birthday and thereafter is older than that age. Thus if legislation or a rule says *"a person over age 16,"* technically it means a person who is one day over 16, not 17 years of age or older. The expression is often used to mean the latter rather than the former. To eliminate the ambiguity say *"16 or over"* if it is intended to include 16 year olds, or *"17 or over"* if it is intended to exclude 16 year olds. Lack of clarity can be created at the end of an age period by saying *"until age 65."* This can mean until a person reaches age 65 or age 66. Eliminate the problem by saying *"under"* the age that is intended to be the cut off point. Thus if it is intended to include persons who have reached their 18th birthday but not their 70th birthday, say *"a person 18 or over but under 70."* It is not necessary to use the words *"age"* or *"years of age"* before or after the number. If it is thought desirable to refer to age—say *"age 18"* rather than *"18 years of age"* because the former is shorter.

O. CAPITAL LETTERS

The same rule applies to both capital letters and hyphens—do not use them unless required for the sake of clarity. As a general rule, capitalize only the first word in a sentence and proper nouns. Do not capitalize branches or departments of government or a private entity (*the general assembly, department of revenue, board of directors*) or offices (*the governor, the chief justice, chief financial officer*).

P. HYPHENS

A hyphen is used to indicate a word compounded of two or more words to represent a single idea. It should not be used because its proper usage is only temporary. One authority has stated that "[t]wo or more words which represent a single idea may stand as separate words or become hyphenated or be written as one word. The usual sequence is for the words to be written separate at first, then to become hyphenated, and finally to be written solid. The overall rule is to avoid ambiguity."[14] The drafter should not waste time trying to ascertain which stage the particular combination of words is at when drafting. Because most documents, legislation, and rules are effective indefinitely unless repealed, the drafter should not adopt a usage that is only temporary. As between using two words combined or separate, use the one that is the most common. If in doubt, use two words.

Endnotes

1. R. Flesch, The Art of Plain Talk 81–91 (1946).

2. R. Flesch, supra note 1, at 81, uses the terms "full words" and "empty words." I prefer Wydick's terminology and use it in the text. R. Wydick, Plain English for Lawyers 9 (4th ed. 1998).

3. W. Strunk, Jr. and E. White, The Elements of Style 24, 42, 53 (4th ed. 2000).

4. Id; R. Dickerson, The Fundamentals of Legal Drafting 209–213 (2d ed. 1986); R. Flesch, supra note 1 at 82–83 (1946); E. Gowers, The Complete Plain Words 54–56 (Rev. ed. 1986); R. Wydick, supra note 2 at 10–12.

5. Professor David Mellinkoff has shown the fallacy of this argument in all but a few instances in his book The Language of the Law 345–66 (1963).

6. "As if plain words, useful and intelligible instructions, were not as good for an esquire, or one that is in commission from the King, as for him that holds the plough." John Eachard, The Grounds and Occasions of the Contempt of the Clergy and Religion enquired into (1670) quoted on the copyright page of E. Gowers, supra note 4.

7. R. Flesch, How to Write Plain English 9 (1979).

8. R. Dickerson, supra note 4, at 27.

9. R. Wydick, supra note 2, at 74.

10. R. Flesch, supra note 7, at 102–113. Dickerson's rebuttal is in his book Materials on Legal Drafting 285–88 (1981).

11. It should be noted that in some jurisdictions, most notably California, the tabulation drafting style is to set out each tabulated line as a complete sentence, whether it is a complete sentence or a fragment. The disadvantage of this approach is that is grammatically incorrect. The reason this approach has been adopted in California (and elsewhere, for example Alabama) is the belief that the section is easier to read and results in fewer errors when the section is amended. If the California style is used, there is no need for an "and" or an "or" preceding the last item in the series, but there is a need to determine if all or only one of the series applies. The "California style" is included in the appendix to provide an example of this alternative approach.

12. Although this principle was once a standard rule of grammar, it has fallen into disfavor. Strunk and White, however, still recommend it. W. Strunk, Jr. and E. White, supra note 3, at 2.

13. 2A Sutherland, Statutes and Statutory Construction 405751.08 (4th ed. rev. 1984).

14. M. Shertzer, The Elements of Grammar 109 (1986).

Chapter 9

AMBIGUITY, VAGUENESS, AND GENERALITY

A. IMPORTANCE OF UNDERSTANDING WHAT THEY ARE AND THE DIFFERENCES BETWEEN THEM

In any type of legal drafting, the drafter must be aware that the purpose of the document is to communicate the ideas the drafter has, whether generated by the drafter or the client, to others. It is seldom that a legal document is solely for the use of the drafter. Depending upon the type of legal document the drafter is preparing, the audience can include the immediate client, employees, a governmental agency, a legislative body, the public, and ultimately the courts. To do this effectively and avoid the possibility for misunderstanding, the drafter must be aware of three major problem areas of language and the major differences between them that are of particular concern to the legal drafter. These three are ambiguity, vagueness, and generality.

B. AMBIGUITY[1]

The best known and probably the most misunderstood of the three problem areas is ambiguity. Concern with ambiguity has reached a point that the term is used to mean not only ambiguity itself but also vagueness, generality, and the failure of a statute, rule, or legal document to address an issue.[2] There are three types of ambiguity:

1. Semantic. According to Dickerson, the most serious problem of language is ambiguity in the traditional sense of equivocation. A word is equivocal when it has more than one definition. This type of ambiguity arose in the 2004 federal election when federal law allowed a voter whose qualifications to vote were challenged to cast a provisional ballot in the jurisdiction where the voter claimed to be registered. Disputes arose over whether "jurisdic-

tion" meant precinct, county, or even state. The term "residence" is a constant problem because it can mean physical, legal, voting, or permanent residence. Context can often but not always solve a problem of semantic ambiguity. This type of ambiguity is to be distinguished from homonyms—words that are spelled the same but have different meanings depending on context (A can can be recycled if put in a garbage can).

2. Syntactic. A syntactic ambiguity is one that arises when there is uncertainty what a word modifies or refers back to in the statute, rule, or legal document. The first type is the "squinty modifier, e.g. "when the governor nominates the head of a department, he shall appear before the committee that oversees that department." While the requirement of a committee appearance probably applies only to the nominee, it could mean the governor. The potential for confusion is easily eliminate if the "he" is replaced by "the nominee". The second occurs when a modifier precedes or follows a series of nouns, e.g. "to a charitable corporation or an institution performing an educational function." In this example it is not clear whether "educational function" applies to all charitable corporations or only to institutions that perform an educational function. The problem can usually be solved by tabulation if the modifier is intended to apply both types of institutions. If intended to apply only to the last noun in the series, add a comma before that noun and add "to" before it and each other noun in the series (to a charitable corporation, or to an institution performing an educational function).

3. Contextual. Contextual ambiguity arises when it is unclear which of two or more available alternatives is intended. The ambiguity can explicit or implicit, and internal or external. There is an explicit internal ambiguity when a statute, rule, or legal document imposing a duty refers in one section to "persons" and in another to "residents" or in one section to filing a document within 30 days and in another to filing the same document within 60 days, without any obvious reason for the difference. The explicit ambiguity is external if the differences are in different statutes, rules, or legal documents. Creating more problems is an implicit contextual ambiguity. This occurs when one or more but not all members of a class are mentioned, leaving it up to the reader to decide whether the omission was intentional or accidental. The canon of construction *"expressio unius est exclusio alterius."* as developed to cover some of these situations but as is shown in chapter 12 it, as with all canons of construction, does not determine how a statute will be construed in any individual case but merely provides a basis for justifying the construction adopted.

C. CONFUSING AMBIGUITY WITH OTHER DRAFT-ING PROBLEMS

While the concern for improving the quality of the drafting of statutes, rules, and legal documents has been a positive development in recent years, there has been an increasing tendency to label any drafting defect as creating an ambiguity. The first and best known was Arthur Miller"s article about the advantages of purposive ambiguity. In this article words that Miller labeled as ambiguous were nothing more than vague terms such as "reasonable" and "due process". An even more egregious misuse of the ambiguity label was by Federal Courts Study Committee. In its Final Report in 1990 at pp. 155–56 it lists 15 recommendations for eliminating statutory ambiguities. An examination of the list shows that 14 of them concern the simple failure of a statute to address a subject such as the applicable statute of limitations. The fifteenth concerned providing definitions of key terms, a problem of vagueness or generality. None concerned ambiguity. Compounding the problem was an article about the report published two years later. In the article the author reports on his survey of U.S. Supreme Court decisions that showed 20 recurring ambiguities in statutes construed by the Court.[3] An examination of that list shows that 17 are nothing more than the failure of a statute to address an issue, two were generality problems, and one of vagueness. None was an ambiguity problem. Failure to address an issue comes closest to an implied internal or external contextual ambiguity, but in reality it is a separate problem.

Ambiguity in the drafting of statutes, rules, and legal documents is a problem, The problem will not be solved, however, by labeling every drafting mistake, especially those that are the failure to include a necessary provision, as an ambiguity.

D. VAGUENESS

Vagueness is often confused with semantic ambiguity but in fact they are quite different. While semantic ambiguity is concerned with a word that has two or more definitions (resident), vagueness is concerned with the uncertainty resulting from the broadness of the term (person, student, employer, voter, operator). With ambiguity the choice of which definition to use is central to the construction of the term and is usually an "either-or" question, while with vagueness the issue is not central but at the margins, a question of degree. Most words that denote classes or categories have elements of vagueness (employer, property, adjacent), as do concepts (reasonable, due process, equal). When commentators speak of intentional or purposive ambiguity and especially when they say it may be desirable, what they are talking about is vagueness, leaving it up to administrative agencies or the courts to work out the precise parameters of the term.

E. GENERALITY

A word is classified as general when it is not limited to a unique person or thing and thus can denote more than one, i.e. when it refers to a class, e.g. grandparent (paternal, maternal), parent (natural, adoptive), child (natural, adoptive, legitimate, illegitimate), property (real, personal, intangible, residential, commercial). It is different from ambiguity in that it permits simultaneous reference while ambiguity permits only alternative reference. A general term can, for the purposes of the legal drafter, over inclusive or under inclusive and thus requires great care on the part of the drafter to be neither.

F. DISTINGUISHING BETWEEN VAGUENESS AND GENERALITY

As can be seen from sections C and D above, the definitions of vagueness and generality given by Dickerson overlap because they each include classes of persons, things, or actions. The legal drafter should be more precise in distinguishing between the two so as to be more precise in choosing the word that most clearly expresses the drafter's intent. The proper distinctions are:

1. Vagueness. A vague word can be:

   a. descriptive—near, intentional, material, adjacent, high, low, handicapped, impaired, injured, due process, equal protection, restraint of trade, reasonable;

   b. an action—give, sell, provide, inform, assist, conspire, injure, solicit, display;

   c. a concept—freedom, liberty, religion, strength, fear, growth, beauty, art, music.

2. Generality. A general word is a noun that includes a class that is comprised of persons or things—parent, child, employer, neighbor, friend, enemy, country, plant, tree, animal, dog, house, building.

G. ELIMINATING AMBIGUITY, UNINTENDED VAGUENESS, AND OVER AND UNDER GENERALITY

Being aware of the difficulties that can be caused by ambiguity, vagueness, or over or under generality is the first step for the legal drafter but not the last. For ambiguity, the best way to eliminate most forms of it is to use the drafting techniques set forth in this book, especially chapters 5–8. Using the singular number, active voice, and the present tense, and gender neutral drafting will do wonders in eliminating syntactic ambiguity. Following good drafting techniques, however, cannot eliminate unintended vagueness and over or under generality.

Rather their elimination requires the legal drafter to know the intention of the person or body for whom the drafting is being done, being conscious of the consequences of using the wrong word, and being precise in choosing the correct word. In other words, legal drafting requires the highest degree of professionalism.

Endnotes

1. Sections B, D, and E are drawn from Chapter 3 of R. Dickerson, The Fundamentals of Legal Drafting (2d ed. 1996).

2. Miller, Statutory Language and the Purposive Use of Ambiguity, 42 Va. L. Rev. 39 (1956).

3. Maggs, Reducing the Costs of Statutory Ambiguity: Alternative Approaches and the Federal Courts Study Committee, 29 Harvard J. on Legislation 123, 143–48 (1998).

Part IV

DISTINCTIVE ASPECTS OF DRAFTING LEGISLATION

Chapter 10

THE LEGISLATIVE PROCESS

A. IMPORTANCE TO DRAFTER

The legislative process is important to the drafter of legislation in a variety of ways. The drafter should be familiar in general terms with the process by which a bill (or other legislative instrument) the drafter prepares becomes a law so that the drafter understands the context in which it will be considered. More specifically, the process determines the different audiences for the bill before it becomes a law.

The initial audience is the proponent of the bill, that is the person, group, or body that requests the drafter to prepare the bill. This can be an individual legislator, a private client, a private group such as a bar association or public interest organization, a public study group such as a legislative or governmental committee, or a government agency or official. The next audience, if the proponent is not a legislator, is the one or more legislators who will be asked to introduce the bill, and their staffs. During consideration by a legislative committee, the immediate audience is the members of the committee, their staffs, and the staff of the committee. When considered by either house of the legislature, the members of that house and their staffs are those most concerned. After passage, the executive whose approval is required and the executive's staff are the focus. Once the bill is signed, the members of the public affected by the act, governmental agencies and officials who will administer it, and courts that will interpret and apply it are the audience.

Of course, if the bill drafting process is public, or being considered in the legislative process from introduction through approval by the executive, the bill has an audience much broader than the immediate audience. Depending upon the importance of the bill and its impact on public and private interests, the bill may be of concern to legislators, governmental bodies or officials, other legislative committees, the news media, special interest groups, public and private groups, and the staffs, their advisors, and attorneys of each individual group, or body. At every step in the process, the language of the bill will be read, studied, and debated by those in the immediate audience and the broader audience. In the drafting process, the drafter must be aware of these various audiences and prepare the draft so that it can be easily read and understood by the members of each. It is not enough to draft only for the proponent who is the initial audience.

The drafter must also understand the legislative process sufficiently so that the drafter can comply with the technical or formal requirements that are applicable to the process. These requirements are in the rules of each legislative body as well as in the applicable constitution and statutes, discussed in chapter 4.

B. SOURCES OF PROPOSED LEGISLATION

Although only a member of the legislative body can introduce a bill into the formal legislative process, the individual legislator is seldom the drafter of the bill. Usually someone else arranges for the drafting because that someone else is the real proponent of the substance of the legislation. As noted in the previous section, the proponent who requests a drafter to prepare a bill can range from a private individual to a legislative committee. In theory, anyone can draft a bill and ask a legislator to introduce it. In practice, it often works that way. Even a legislator who wants to introduce a bill may not have to draft the bill personally or even have it done by a member of the legislator's staff. Congress and most state legislatures have legislative drafting agencies that provide bill drafting services for their members. The services of these agencies are generally available only to members and those who have a formal relationship to the legislature. In some states, however, a bill cannot be introduced by a legislator until it has been reviewed by the legislative drafting agency to ensure that the bill meets the technical requirements as to form.

Legislation at the local level—county, city, township, or special district—has the same sources but only the largest counties or munici-palities have a separate ordinance drafting office. In most local govern-ments, ordinance drafting is done by whatever office or person provides legal counsel to the legislative body, usually the county or city attorney.

C. THE LEGISLATIVE PROCESS

Although the legislative process in a particular legislative body is usually referred to in the singular, there are in fact two separate legislative processes in each legislature. The first is the formal legislative process. This is established in the rules of the legislative body, some of which may be dictated by constitutional provisions for Congress and state legislatures, or by statute or charter for local governmental bodies. It is essentially the same for every bill and thus can be described and even diagrammed with considerable accuracy. The second is the political legislative process. It is governed not by formal rules but by politics and personalities. It is different for every bill and thus cannot be described or diagrammed in advance but only after action on the bill is completed.

The formal legislative process is set out in diagram form in the next section, one for Congress[1] and one for a typical state legislature.[2] The legislative drafter should be familiar with this process so that the drafter can satisfy its requirements as to form. Beyond that, the drafter should understand the points at which the bill will be considered and may be amended. At any of these stages the drafter may be called upon to explain the bill's provisions, to draft amendments, or even to rewrite the entire bill. The drafter should also be aware that at any stage other persons may prepare amendments or revisions that will affect the drafter's handiwork.

The formal legislative process begins with the introduction of a bill by a legislator. The introduction is made by filing the bill with the appropriate officer of the legislature or in a place designated for that purpose. In Congress, it is a "hopper" placed next to the clerk's desk in the chamber of each house. Upon introduction, the bill is referred to a committee of the legislature by a person or committee assigned that responsibility. The person may be a member or an officer such as the speaker, or a nonmember officer such as the clerk. Usually this process is mechanical, but it can sometimes be political if the assignor may appropriately refer the bill to one of several different committees. Controversy may arise if one of the committees may be more or less favorably disposed toward the bill, the assignor wishes to help or hinder the passage of the bill, and makes the assignment on that basis.

The drafter must, of course, also be aware of the political legislative process. This is the process that determines how far the bill will go through the formal legislative process. It will also determine the extent to which the bill will be amended as it moves through the formal process and by whom the language of any amendment will be drafted. An important part of the drafting of a bill is to weigh the political implications of its various provisions. On each potentially controversial issue, the proponent will have to make a choice whether to modify the provisions of the bill in an effort to maximize support or minimize opposition, and how that choice will be reflected in the bill. In many instances the drafter is in the best position to identify the areas in which choices must be made and to bring them to the attention of the proponent.

The legislative process thus affects the drafting of a bill in two ways. In its formal sense, it controls the form and style of the bill and establishes the framework for the consideration of the bill and the steps at which the bill can be killed or amended. In its political sense, it may affect the substance of the bill. Both affect the drafter in that they determine what the drafter puts in the bill.

Some argue that the study of legislation should focus on what I have characterized as the political legislative process. They contend that to construe legislation, a lawyer or court must have thorough understanding of the legislative process.[3] The difficulty with this thesis, however, is that the political legislative process can best be understood by studying the process by which a particular bill was enacted. Our own experience in the legislative process has taught us that the only generalization that can be drawn from the study of the fate of a particular bill or a number of bills is that the process is political, compromises are made on almost every piece of legislation enacted, and the real reasons why one bill passes and another does not can never be part of a legislative history on which a court could rely. For these reasons, only the formal legislative process is set out in detail in the next section. That does not mean the political process is not important or that the drafter should ignore it, but only that there are too many variables in it to permit it to be summarized or diagrammed except in retrospect as to a bill that has either passed or failed to pass.

D. A DIAGRAM OF THE FORMAL LEGISLATIVE PROCESS

Set out below are two diagrams of a legislative process. The first outlines the process in the Congress of the United States. The second is for a typical state legislature. The latter is based on the Ohio legislature, but the process in other state legislatures is essentially the same. Local legislative bodies are almost always unicameral, and thus there is no consideration in a second house and no conference committees. Similarly, in many local legislatures, the executive is a member of the legislative body or presides over it. The executive may or may not have the power to veto legislative action.

THE FEDERAL PROCESS

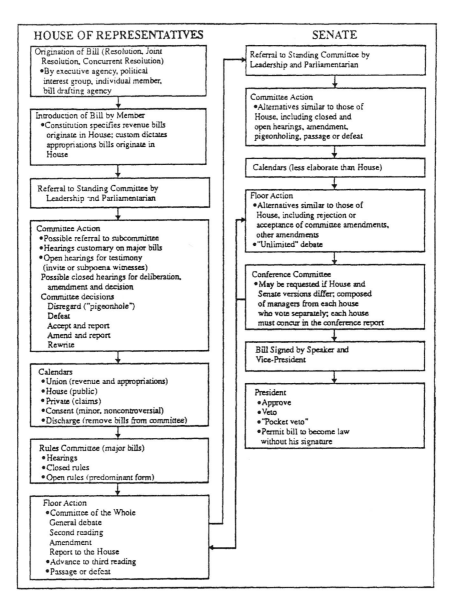

Source: W. Keefe and M. Ogul, The American Legislative Process (10th ed. 2001). Reprinted by permission of Pearson Education, Inc., Upper Saddle River, N.J.

TYPICAL STATE PROCESS

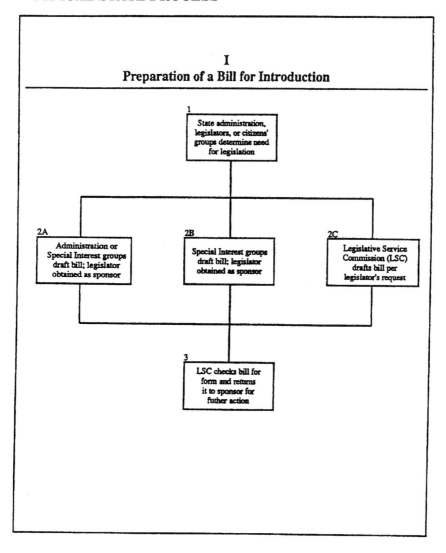

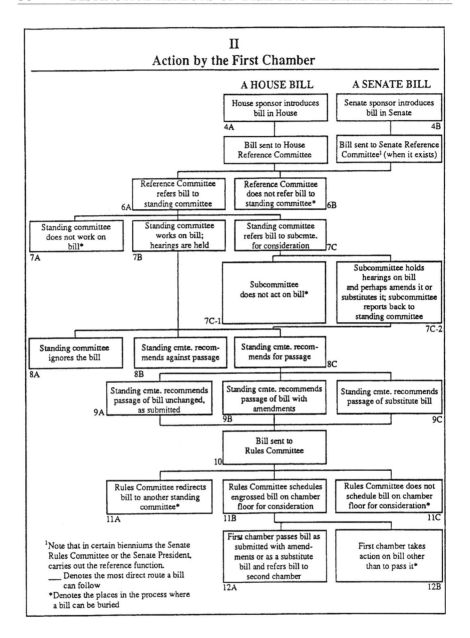

Source: R. Sheridan, *Governing Ohio: The State Legislature* (1988). Used with permission.

Endnotes

1. The formal legislative process in the U.S. congress is described in a booklet entitled How Our Laws Are Made. It is published anew for each congress by the house of representatives. The current edition was revised and updated by Edward F. Wellett, Jr., Law Revision counsel of the house and published in late 1989 as House Document No. 101–139. A broader look at both the formal and political process in congress and in the states is found in W. Keefe and M. Ogul, The American Legislative Process (10th ed. 2001) and J. Davis, Legislative Law and Process (2d ed. 1986).

2. Each state legislature usually publishes a short description of its formal process. In many states private groups or authors have published descriptions of both the formal and political processes. A good example is R. Sheridan, Governing Ohio: The State Legislature (1989). For a detailed description of the legislative process in California, see E. Dotson, California's Legislature (2000), especially ch. IX.

3. Mikva, Reading and Writing Statutes, 48 U. of Pittsburgh L. Rev. 627 (1987); Lane, Legislative Process and Its Judicial Renderings: A Study in Contrast, 48 U. of Pittsburgh L. Rev. 639, 639–42 (1987); Posner, Statutory Interpretation—in the Classroom and in the Courtroom, 50 U. of Chicago L. Rev. 800, 802 (1983).

Chapter 11

LEGISLATIVE DRAFTING PROCESS

A. MOST DIFFICULT FORM OF DRAFTING

Legislative drafting has been called the "most difficult form of drafting" by Dickerson "because, while the basic problems of drafting are the same, legislative problems are technically more complicated and socially more important." He also quoted Middleton Beaman, the late Counsel of the United States House of Representatives, as saying that "the number of contingencies that a lawyer has to guard against in the case of a will or contract, while sometimes very numerous, are mere flyspecks compared with the contingencies that must be considered in the case of a statute."[1]

Stated differently, an error in a simple contract between two people will affect the parties that enter into the contract. An error in a simple legislative proposal if enacted will affect thousands or, quite possibly, millions of people subject to the law.

The consequences of an error in legislation are also broader and vary from state to state. An extreme example is in states that follow the "enrolled bill rule." This rule prevents a court from considering an acknowledged drafting error when construing a statute if the bill was properly authenticated when sent to the executive for consideration.[2] On the federal level, an error or omission resulting in litigation may or may not lead to the result intended by Congress.[3] As stated in chapter 11, clear and unambiguous drafting is the most effective way to force a court to construe the statute in a manner consistent with the proponent's intent.

B. KNOW THE POLICY OBJECTIVE OF THE CLIENT

"A statute is the formal and legal expression of a legislative policy and it follows that before a statute can be drafted the policy sought to be implemented by it must be determined."[4]

Before beginning to craft a legislative proposal, the drafter must clearly understand the policy objectives of the person requesting the legislation. It is helpful to have an understanding of the problem the legislation seeks to address. Like all forms of legal drafting, the suggestions presented in chapter 3 in the discussion regarding the legal drafter as architect, builder and journalist in determining the client's goal apply to drafting legislation.[5] By engaging in a dialogue with the client, very much like the conversations necessary in drafting other legal documents, the drafter will clarify the goal of the drafting assignment, the complexities in achieving that goal, and the various alternatives.

At times, the legislative drafter will simply be presented with a simple declarative statement of what change the client would like in law. At other times, the drafter will be presented with a complete draft of the changes in law the client believes can be accomplished.[6] Legislative drafting is a collaborative process, where the drafter consults with the client to discuss the result sought by the proposed change in law, policy, and legal issues raised by that change, and alternative methods of achieving the intended result. If the client does not know the law, but simply wants to alter a practice, it is the drafter's role to educate the client.

C. UNDERSTAND THE POLITICAL NATURE OF THE TASK

The legislative process is a political process and drafting legislation cannot be separated from its political nature.

"Legislatures are political bodies, and the provision of any number of technical services will not change their essentially political character. The finest draftsmanship in the world cannot bring about the adoption of wise legislative policies if the elected members of a representative body are mediocrities or worse. In fact, the professional legislative draftsman regards himself strictly as a technician and not as a policy-maker in his own right. But legislative research and drafting work that is thorough and technically sound can contribute notably to wise legislative decision. By careful analysis and clear presentation of policy alternatives, the skilled draftsman can narrow the area of partisan disagreement on any bill and make possible an on-the-merits consideration of noncontroversial issues and provisions. And, whatever one's views on a particular legislative policy, a statute that is well-drafted technically and carefully tailored to the provisions of existing law is certainly to be preferred to a statute that is both ill-conceived in policy and hurriedly thrown together in expression and form." [7]

With respect to some drafting assignments, it is may be the role of the legislative drafter to present the political choices presented for resolution by the client. It is important to know the initial audience of the legislation, generally the member of the legislature who requested the bill, but often a special interest on whose behalf the request was made. It is also important to know the legislature both as a whole, and its component parts—each house and the committees of each house. The drafter must also consider legislative rules that may affect the introduction or consideration of the legislation.

Part of the drafting process may be determining the best house for bill introduction, and the form in which the bill should be introduced. The draft of the bill will often dictate the committee to which it is assigned. One committee may be preferable to another. For example, a bill that prohibits the use of cartoon characters in advertisements for products that are harmful to the health of children may be heard in the Health Committee, which may be more sympathetic to public health issues, or the Judiciary Committee, which may be more sympathetic to the commercial interests of the producer. How the bill is drafted can impact the bill assignment and its success.

The legal drafter needs to be knowledgeable about other parties with an interest in the subject matter, such as lobbyists representing special interests and governmental agencies that may have a role in implementation should the legislation be enacted. The drafter should also be aware of the views and preferences of the chief executive who will make the ultimate decision about the legislation after it passes the legislature.

If the bill becomes a statute, the audience will change, and this must also be anticipated at the drafting stage. Will disputes over the language of the statute be resolved in a judicial forum? Have terms used in the legislation been construed by a court? Is that construction helpful or harmful to the intent of the client? Are there alternative terms that may be used to avoid that construction?

Of equal importance is the determination whether the statute will make an intermediate stop at an administrative agency to be further "clarified" by way of administrative regulation. Are there other regulations in existence that may affect the construction of the newly enacted statute?

The legislature drafter should be knowledgeable about these matters and should educate the client. The legislation should be drafted so that if the bill becomes a statute it will express the intent of the proponents and be construed by the administrative agency and the court in a manner consistent with that intent.

D. MORE THAN A SCRIBE

As can be seen from the foregoing, a legislative drafter is more than a scribe. How much more than a scribe the legislative drafter will be is determined by the nature of the client-drafter relationship, the degree of experience each possesses, and the drafting assignment. David Marcello points out that at all stages of the drafting process—determining the client's intent, setting drafting priorities, evaluating alternatives, selecting the legislative instrument, and allocating discretion—all involve value laden choices. Marcello recommends that legislative "drafters be aware of the many points at which their personal and political views may be influential in the drafting process and that they take steps to minimize such influence," but not deny that there are "opportunities to inject personal judgments into the process." [8]

When drafting legislation, the drafter may identify policy disagreements that must be resolved. The drafter may be in the best position to draw together the various interests to resolve these policy differences. In identifying issues and conferring with the various interests, the drafter necessarily becomes involved in the policy discussion. The drafter also contributes to policy determinations through the discretion exercised in addressing the numerous minor details that need to be resolved. Often, the client is not available or does not have an interest in the level of detail the drafter must achieve to produce a comprehensive draft.

In the final analysis, whether the legislative drafter has avoided interjecting personal policy judgment into the assignment will be apparent to the client when the client reviews the work product. It is important that the drafter understand the role of the drafter and consult with the client when a policy judgment is needed to ensure that either the client makes the final decision or delegates that power to the drafter.

E. DELIBERATE VAGUENESS AND GENERALITY

While some forms of ambiguity discussed in chapter 9 often result from poor drafting, vagueness and generality in legislation are often deliberate due to the political nature of the legislative process. Sometimes the perfect legislative resolution of a particular issue is not politically possible. Yet, the participants in the legislative process do not easily concede defeat and prefer to declare partial victory.

For political reasons, a client may either refuse to address vagueness or generality in a draft to which the legislative drafter draws the client's attention or may ask the drafter to insert vague or overly general language in the draft as a way of glossing over controversies for which consensus is not reached. Failing to address adequately issues raised by the legislation or avoiding points of controversy can result in the enactment of a statute that is incomplete, vague, or overly general, and that delegates to an administrative agency or a court, or both, the ability to ultimately decide its full meaning. The meaning may not be the meaning intended by the legislature. This outcome can occur despite a drafter's best intention to draft a measure in a comprehensive manner.

The legislative drafter is often blamed for deficiencies in drafting. This blame is well placed when the draft is unintentionally vague or overly general. However, the drafter is also blamed for vagueness or generality in the draft that the drafter was directed to insert and is generally powerless to respond to this accusation because of the confidentiality associated with preparing legislation for clients.

F. TIME PRESSURE

"It may be supposed from my description that the drafting of legislation is a leisurely process, but unfortunately it is not. Rarely is a bill prepared under ideal conditions; usually the work must be done in a hurry and under pressure. One of the main reasons is that few people realize how much is involved in the preparation of legislation, with the result that insufficient time is allowed." [9]

Most legal drafting tasks have deadlines and often there is time pressure associated with those time constraints. A noteworthy aspect of drafting legislation is the additional time pressure associated with drafting during a legislative session. Part time legislatures meet for short periods of time during which they attempt to accomplish the work of the entire session. Full time legislatures meet only for prescribed periods of time. All legislatures adhere to "calendars" that specify when a bill may be heard and by which date a bill must clear a legislative obstacle, such as the policy or fiscal committee deadline or passage from the house of origin to the second house. Generally, bills are introduced at the beginning of session. All bills must be resolved by the end of the session. These time constraints cause an initial crush of requests for legislation early in the session. As bills work their way through the process and deadlines become imminent, there is another wave of requests to amend these bills. Finally, it is typical for the majority of bills to be heard on the floor of the houses during the last days of the session. While these legislative deadlines were intended to evenly spread out the hearing and consideration of bills throughout the entire session, in reality they result in additional logjams.

During deadline periods it is not unusual for a professional legislative drafter to have multiple requests due at the same time. When a bill is being heard on the floor and is in jeopardy of failing passage, there is often a last minute effort to amend the bill. There is no other time pressure quite like the experience of having the speaker of the house or the president pro tempore of the senate standing over the drafter's shoulder and imploring the drafter to complete the task because the house is in session, the members are on the floor, and the process has ground to a halt awaiting the amendments.

G. PLACEMENT OF THE LEGISLATION

"A statute drafted without sufficient attention to legislation already on the books and to the state of the relevant judge-made law inevitably raises vexing problems of interpretation. Issues of federal and state constitutional law have a way of popping up in connection with the simplest sounding statutory proposal."[10]

In addition to the suggestions provided in chapter 3 regarding generally "knowing the law," the legislative drafter must also consider broad constitutional issues such as equal protection and due process, as well as issues such as preemption or the legislative body's authority to act. The drafter must be aware of the constitutional provisions that govern the enactment of statutes in the drafter's jurisdiction, such as title and enacting clause requirements, and single subject and other content restrictions mentioned in chapter 12.

The legislative drafter must also know the specific substantive law and its framework as it relates to the drafting assignment and where the legislative proposal fits into the existing structure of law. As Driedger explains, the drafter "must consider a statute in its relation to other statutes and the law generally, . . . [, and should regard the] statute as one fragment of a much greater whole and any new law must of course be in harmony with existing law."[11]

Finally, the legislative drafter must be knowledgeable about the administrative and decisional law adopted in the drafter's jurisdiction that might affect the interpretation of the language used in crafting the legislation.

Once conversant with the substantive law and its framework, the legislative drafter must determine what changes to existing law are needed to address problems or conflicts the proposed revision of law may create.

Even with years of experience in a particular substantive area of law, it is often the case that the legislative drafter does not possess sufficient expertise for the drafting assignment and will need to conduct additional research. This research should start with identifying the subject matter and the code that contains the subject matter (which can be done by simply beginning with the table of contents of that code) to identify the proper placement of the proposal.[12] Fortunately, legislatures keep records of previously introduced legislation and few ideas are truly new but are simply a variation on an idea that was not successful in an earlier attempt. A seasoned bill drafter generally finds a legislative proposal has been introduced in at least one prior session. Legislative indexes and tables of sections affected are invaluable tools to finding previously introduced legislation and are helpful in providing guidance when drafting the new proposal because they guide the drafter to related legislation and current law.

Treatises on the subject matter may also be consulted to give the legislative drafter a more thorough understanding of existing law and of how the proposal will alter that law. Typically, that legislative drafters work with others engaged in the same task, draft for individuals who have some knowledge about the subject matter, and have access to committee consultants who are experts in the particular area of law. The drafter should make use of these resources; to the extent the drafter is not limited by other considerations.[13]

Once the substantive area of law and its framework are identified, the legislative drafter must determine if the requested legislation requires an addition to, or amendment or repeal of, that law.[14]

Because of the unique conditions of legislative drafting, the drafter should be mindful that sometimes an earlier enactment may have been drafted in haste and provisions of law may have been inserted in an illogical or incorrect place in the code. For example, if the client wants to enact a law that relates to the consolidation of all elections, requiring that city, regional, and statewide elections all occur on the same day, the provision should be placed in part of the code that relates to all elections. The drafter should also check the parts of the elections code that relate to each political subdivision to see if the timing of elections is addressed in these subparts and needs to be amended.

Continuing with the example of election timing, assume that in a prior session during the early hours of the morning as the session was approaching its final hour, an amendment was drafted "on the floor" that placed a provision that related to all elections in the part of the code that governs only city elections. This example is drawn to make two points. First, proper placement of a particular provision is critical not only to the task at hand but to law that will subsequently be enacted. Second, when drafting legislation, it is important to examine the code to find its most appropriate placement and, if time allows and the current client permits, to correct earlier enacted statutes that may have been improperly placed and relates to the current drafting assignment.

H. USE OF MODEL LEGISLATION, PREVIOUSLY INTRODUCED BILLS, AND OTHER ENACTMENTS AS DRAFTING "FORMS"

In most instances it is not necessary for a legislative drafter to "start from scratch" with each new drafting assignment. Just as forms in other types of legal drafting can be helpful, existing proposals may be used as forms when drafting legislation. Generally, entities such as the National Conference of the Commissioners on Uniform State Laws and the American Law Institute draft model acts of very high quality. It is likely there are countless similar bills in the drafter's jurisdiction that were introduced but not enacted in prior sessions. Additionally, there are enactments in other jurisdictions on the same or a similar subject matter that may be helpful to the drafter.

It is often helpful to review these various sources for similar legislation that may be relevant. When using a model act, an enactment from another jurisdiction, or a prior bill on the same or similar subject as a starting point for drafting, the general admonition on the use of forms applies. First, the drafter should apply the principles of proper drafting to the document. Second, the drafter should tailor the document to the particular drafting assignment. Third, the drafter should thoroughly check the document for accuracy to determine if related law has changed in the jurisdiction since the document was drafted.

Nonetheless, using these sources as forms can be useful as a research tool in identifying existing law, bringing to the drafter's attention necessary components of the legislation that may not have occurred to the drafter, and as a template for the current drafting assignment.

I. PREPARE A PLAN, FIRST DRAFT, AND REVISIONS

The considerations identified in chapter 3 regarding preparing a plan, preparing a first draft, and making revisions apply when drafting legislation. The legislative drafter should consult with that chapter for more information on these topics.

J. USE A CHECKLIST, AND WRITE AND ANNOTATE A DIGEST OF THE PROPOSAL

Once satisfied with the first draft and its revisions, the legislative drafter should develop a checklist to determine if the formal requirement of the bill necessary to introduce the bill and have it go into effect if enacted, have been satisfied (such as those specified in chapter 12). The checklist might include some of the following.

__Does the title include all of the provisions of the bill and accurately describe how the bill changes existing law (amendment, addition, and repeal)?

__Does the relating clause encompass the entire contents of the bill?

__If applicable, do the entire contents of the bill fall within a single subject?

__Does the draft include an enacting clause?

__If amending an existing statute, did the drafter use the last amended form of that statute?

__Are there terms used in the bill that should be defined?

__Are the statutory references accurate and do they use the most current form of the statute?

__Are cross references in the bill accurate?

__Did the drafter follow the principles of writing in plain English so that the language that clearly states the legislation's intent?

__Do the contents of the bill follow in logical sequence?

__Does the bill need a provision regarding its operation, such as an emergency (or urgency) clause that will cause the bill to take immediate effect upon enactment?

The legislative drafter should also check the substance of the bill for completeness and accuracy. Preparing a digest of the legislation may be helpful in accomplishing this goal.[15] A digest is a brief summary of existing law and an explanation of changes the legislation would make to that law. The digest should start with a general statement of the existing law followed by a point by point summary of the specific provisions of existing law and the changes the bill would make to that law. The digest, once written, should be annotated with specific citations to existing law (following the statement of existing law) and a specific citation to each section of the bill (following the statement of what the bill would do).

Continuing with the example of an elections code bill relating to the timing of elections, a digest might read as follows:

> Existing law specifies the day on which elections may be held [Cite to the general provisions of the Elections Code that specifies the timing of elections.] Existing law requires that city elections be held on the day provided for in the city charter or on the same day as the statewide election if the charter does not specify a date. [Cite the specific section of the Elections Code that specifies the day for city elections.] Existing law also provides with respect to regional elections that governing board of the regional government may hold the election either on the date of the city election in the city with the greatest population or on the date of a statewide election. [Cite the specific section of the Elections Code that specifies this alternative for regional elections.] Existing law requires that statewide elections be held on the first Tuesday following the first Monday of the month of November in even numbered years. [Cite the specific section that specifies the day on which statewide elections are held.]

> This bill would require that city elections and regional elections be held on the same day as statewide elections. [Cite to the particular sections of the bill that makes these changes.] The bill would also conform related provisions to this requirement. [Cite to other provisions of the bill that make related changes.]

Drafting a digest helps confirm that all of the law necessary to change is included in the legislation. Additionally, the digest provides a check that each section does what the legal drafter intended it to do and that the bill does not have unnecessary provisions.

K. SHOW THE DRAFT TO COLLEAGUES, REVISE DRAFT, PREPARE FINAL DRAFT

The legislative drafter should also follow the advice stated in Chapter 3 about showing the draft to colleagues, revising the draft, preparing the final draft, showing it to the client, and preparing the final document.

Endnotes

1. R. Dickerson, How to Write a Law, 31 Notre Dame Lawyer 14 (1955).

2. An act that is properly enrolled, authenticated, and deposited with the Secretary of State, is conclusive evidence of the legislative will at the time of passage with respect to the language used in the statute. See *Planned Parenthood v. Swoap*, 173 Cal. App. 3d 1187 (1985).

3. See Breyer, On the Uses of Legislative History in Interpreting Statutes, 65 S. Cal. L Rev. 845, 850–51 (1992), citing *United States v. Falvey*, 676 F.2d 871 (1st Cir. 1982) and discussing where the unintentional omission of the words *"current in the United States or in actual use and circulation as money within the United States"* resulted in a possible construction of a revised counterfeiting statute being applied all currency, not just U.S. currency. The court limited the application of the statute to U.S. Currency only after a thorough examination of the legislative history of the bill. The use of legislative history to construe statutes is a practice that under strong criticism. See Kolby, The Supreme Court's Declining Reliance on Legislative History: The Impact of Justice Scalia's Critique, 36 Harv. J. Legislation 369 (1999).

4. Driedger, The Preparation of Legislation, 31 Canadian Bar Rev. 36 (1953).

5. Especially, that the client may not have a clear idea about the legislative proposal.

6. Driedger, supra note 4 at 41: "As a rule a draftsman does not like to receive his instructions in the form of a draft bill: he prefers them in the form of a plain statement of what is intended, supplemented by oral discussion. If he receives a draft, he must construe and interpret what may be an imperfect statement, and may misunderstand what is intended. A draftsman who is presented with a draft measure would not be discharging his duties if he assumed that a proper legislation plan had been conceived and that proper provisions had been chosen to carry it out.... The drafting of legislation does not consist of mere outward polishing.... As a rule no time is saved by preparing a draft bill for submission to the draftsman. When this is done the sponsors often expect that a final draft will be returned the same day or, at the latest, the following day, which is usually the deadline day. Even assuming that a perfect bill is submitted to the draftsman, he must still subject it to the complete drafting process, for how else can he discover that it is a perfect bill and satisfy himself that it will give legislative effect to the intended policy?"

7. Jones, Bill Drafting Services in Congress and the State Legislatures, 65 Harvard L. Rev. 441–442 (1952).

8. Marcello, The Ethics and Politics of Legislative Drafting, 70 Tulane L. Rev. 2437, 2464 (1996). See also Marchant, Representing Representatives: Ethical considerations for the Legislature's Attorneys, 6 N.Y.U. J. Legis. & Pub. Pol'y 439, 461 (2003), discussing that ethical considerations also

include that the legislative drafter, when working as a government lawyer for a legislature, has what Marchant describes as, "several potential clients" in addition to the client making the request, including "the public, the government as a whole, [and] the institution of the legislature.

9. Driedger, supra note 4 at 40.

10. Jones, supra note 7 at 441–442.

11. Driedger, supra note 4 at 37.

12. While it is always refreshing to find logic and order in the codes, as mentioned earlier in this chapter, the legislative process is a political one and decisions about legislation are often made in haste. Revisions of law are sometimes misplaced. When drafting legislation under ideal condition, with adequate time to do thorough research, the drafter should include not only identifying the logical place where the law exists, but also examine related placements to determine if these related provisions also need revision and to "clean up" existing law to make it consistent with the new proposal.

13. For example, the issue of the confidentiality of a proposal may prevent the drafter from contacting and discussing the proposal with the committee consultant, who may be the most knowledgeable person about the subject.

14. Existing law must always be identified and analyzed prior to drafting legislation. However, the form of the legislation will depend on the drafting practice followed in the jurisdiction the legislation will be introduced. At one end of what is a spectrum of methods of preparing legislation, the bill will be a complex revision of existing law that displays the changes to current law by actually revising the text of existing law and requiring no additional work if the bill is enacted. On the other end of the spectrum are those jurisdictions where legislation is a simply declarative statement of how the law should be revised, and if enacted, the revision is integrated into law by a "code revisor," Some jurisdictions follow a hybrid of these two approaches. See G. Grossman, Legal Research, Historical Foundations of the Electronic Age 170–180 (1994).

15. The practice of writing a digest of the bill is required of all bills introduced in the California Legislature (see the Joint Rules of the Senate and Assembly, J.R. 8.5).

Chapter 12

STATUTORY CONSTRUCTION

A. THE DEFINITION OF STATUTORY CONSTRUC-TION

When courts and legislation scholars discuss what happens to a statute after it is enacted, they are usually not concerned with how a statute is interpreted by a lawyer or other interested person reading the statute. They are rather, almost invariably concerned with the process by which a court decides a case upon the basis of a statute. Three labels are usually applied to this process—construction, interpretation, and application. Most often interpretation and construction are used as synonyms.

When a court construes a statute, it actually engages in two separate exercises. First, it must interpret the statute, that is it must determine what the words in the statute mean. Second, it must apply the statute to the facts of the case before it. In the second step, it takes the statute as interpreted and then makes a judgment whether the facts of the case come within its terms. Often a court will not realize that it is engaging in a two step process rather than just one, but that is what happens. An example of this two step process is the interpretation given by the federal courts to 28 U.S.C.A. § 1291. This section provides that federal courts of appeals have jurisdiction over appeals from "final decisions" of the district courts. This statute in one form or another has been in effect since the federal court system was first established in 1789, and has been a source of difficulty to the courts during the entire period. The Supreme Court has interpreted the words "final decisions" to incorporate the "final judgment rule."[1] The court has defined a final judgment as one that ends the litigation on the merits, leaving only execution of the judgment to be completed.[2] Notwithstanding this definition, it has also said that the rule must be applied in a pragmatic rather than a technical way.[3] In line with this approach the court developed the "collateral order" doctrine under which an order is considered as meeting the finality requirement and thus a "final decision" under section 1291 if it

(1) conclusively determines the issue and is not subject to revision; (2) resolves an important issue completely separate from the merits of the case; and (3) is effectively unreviewable upon appeal of the final judgment.[4]

The court was interpreting the phrase "final decisions" when it defined the phrase in terms of the final judgment rule and provided the definition of a final judgment. It was further interpreting "final decisions" when it defined them to include a collateral order, and then gave a definition of a collateral order. Application occurs when a court decides whether a particular order, such as the denial of the certification of a class under Federal Rule of Civil Procedure 23[5] or denial of qualified immunity,[6] is appealable immediately or only after a true final judgment is rendered in the case.

Dickerson does not use the term "construction," and takes a different view as to the distinction between interpretation and application. He defines interpretation to include both interpretation and application when the facts of the case fall within the meaning of the statute as found by the court. Application, on the other hand, he defines as what a court does when it finds that the meaning of the statute does not cover the facts of the case, but the court may still apply it to those facts by using the court's creative function. This occurs when the facts in the case are clearly not within the contemplation of the enacting legislature, but the court thinks that if the legislature had thought of it, the legislature would have wanted the statute to be applied.[7] What Dickerson calls application Judge Richard Posner calls "creative reconstruction," as discussed in chapter 11, section D. Judge Posner, Professsors Eskridge and Frickey, and many legislation scholars use the term interpretation to cover everything a court does with a statute.[8] The author believes the terms "construction," "interpretation," and "application" as they are defined in this section more accurately describe what courts do when faced with the question of the applicability of a statute to a case pending before it.[9]

B. RELATIONSHIP BETWEEN STATUTORY CONSTRUCTION AND LEGISLATIVE DRAFTING

At first blush, it might appear that statutory construction, being concerned with the interpretation and application of statutes already enacted, is of little or no importance to the drafter. Nothing could be further from the truth. If the proponent of the legislation is the initial, immediate audience of the legislation, the courts, which have the final word on what legislation means and how it is to be applied, are its ultimate audience. For this reason it is essential for the drafter to be at least generally familiar with the approaches courts take to statutory construction, how courts use the canons of statutory construction, how courts have construed specific words the drafter may use, and the reliance courts place on the various sources of legislative history. The drafter must be familiar with these subject areas, not because the drafter is likely to be involved when the legislation is interpreted and applied by the courts, but to enable the drafter through careful drafting to prevent the courts from using principles of statutory construction to reach a result not intended by the proponent of the legislation.

The goal of the legislative drafter should be to use language that is so clear and unambiguous that it will force a court construing the statute to construe it the way the proponent intends it to be construed. To the extent that the language used by the drafter is not clear and unambiguous, the door is open for the court to reach a result to which the proponent may object. Knowing how the courts have construed statutory language in the past will help the drafter avoid similar problems in the future. The drafter's goal should be to minimize the occasions when courts find that the language used in a statute is not an adequate expression of legislative intent thus requiring a resort to extraneous aids. If a court has difficulty construing legislation, it usually means the drafter did not draft well.

C. THE PURPOSE OF STATUTORY CONSTRUC-TION

Courts are virtually unanimous in stating that the purpose of statutory construction is to ascertain the intent of the legislature.[10] Scholars of statutory construction are not so sure. One of the most famous criticisms of the "intent" approach to statutory construction challenged the idea that there is or could be any such thing as legislative intent, and that even if there were it would be impossible to ascertain what the intent was.[11] Other critics attempt to distinguish between intent as evidenced by the words used and purpose, arguing that the latter is more important.[12] Still others make a linguistic attack on the plain meaning rule, challenging the idea that words have an accepted meaning, thus making it impossible to know from the words used what was the intent of the legislature.[13] An even more fundamental attack is on the meaning of meaning.[14]

Whatever may be the value of these academic excursions into and behind the purpose of statutory construction, for the drafter of legislation they should remain just that—academic. If the drafter attempted to acquire more than a general familiarity with the scholarship on statutory construction, the drafter would end up with only a headache and a feeling that the entire drafting enterprise is an exercise in futility and not worth the effort.

One distinction that can legitimately be made is between intent and purpose. Intent properly should be limited to interpretation, while purpose has to do with application. To the extent that a legislative body can have an intent, that intent will almost invariably relate to the meaning of the words used in the legislation. The question is properly "What did the legislature mean when it used this word?" This question is essentially definitional, and is answered by the use of more words to explain what was meant by the legislature when it used the word it did. Purpose, on the other hand, comes into play in the application of the legislation to a particular set of facts. Purpose is most relevant when a set of facts is clearly within or without the words of the statute as interpreted by the court, but for reasons beyond the words should or should not be covered by them. A famous example is the statute that made a child the heir of the parent. When a child killed his parent, the question arose whether the statute should be applied so that the child would inherit from the parent he killed, thereby profiting from his own crime. The proper interpretation of the statute was that it did not exclude a child who committed patricide. The court concluded, however, that this result would be contrary to the purpose of the legislature and thus held the child did not inherit.[15] An example of a much broader and more significant application is whether the constitutional guarantee of freedom of the press applies to nonprint media. The term "press," whether it be defined according to original intent or later usage, does not fairly include television or film, but it was easy to apply the term to cover them because of the purpose behind the First Amendment. Similarly, by relying on purpose rather than intent, a statute that made all males eligible to vote also eligible to sit as jurors, passed when only males could vote, could be held to permit female jurors after women were given the right to vote.[16]

The goal of the drafter should be to make the task of a court faced with interpreting and applying legislation as easy as possible. To a large extent this can be done by following the principles of good drafting set forth in chapters 6–9. The primary effect will be on interpretation, but if the legislation or rule is easily interpreted, its application should also be easy.

D. APPROACHES TO STATUTORY CONSTRUCTION

Courts and scholars of legislation have over the years responded to the problems involved in the interpretation and application of statutes by developing various approaches to statutory construction. Some scholars have gone further and attempted to classify the approaches under several broad headings.

Professors Eskridge and Frickey in their casebook on legislation first divide the approaches between "textualist" and "contextual." "Textualist" they define as holding that all or almost all cases can be resolved by reading the statute and applying its plain or most probable meaning to answer questions of interpretation and application. The "contextual" approach, on the other hand, views the textual or plain meaning approach as too limited, and that in a substantial number of cases sources extrinsic to the words of the statute should be examined. Eskridge and Frickey break down the contextual approach into three subclasses. The first is the "legal process" approach of Professors Hart and Sacks that argues unless the words of the statute compel a particular result, courts and others should look to the general purpose of a statute in resolving its interpretation or application. The second they term "economic" because it was developed primarily by Judge Richard Posner, the leading (or at least the most prolific) proponent of the law and economics analysis of the law. The principal feature of this approach is that when a question of interpretation or application is not clearly answered by the text of the statute, a court should through "imaginative reconstruction" decide the question on how the court thinks the legislature that originally enacted the statute would have answered the question. The third approach they term "dynamic" because it argues the meaning of the words of statutes change over time just as the meaning of other words change over time. Under this approach, statutes should not be viewed as determinate and static, and thus the intent or purpose of the enacting legislature is not relevant.[17]

Another author has identified four theoretical approaches, which he labels as deconstruction, conventionalism, public choice theory, and evolutionary constructionism.[18] Posner has written a brief review of the history of statutory construction (he calls it interpretation) starting with Aristotle. Of the more recent approaches, he describes one as "imaginative reconstruction," but he is referring to the Hart and Sacks approach, not his own. Others are the economic, social choice, and hermeneutic. He describes his own approach as moving from economic or interest group to imaginative reconstruction, followed by a command theory, and his most recent, pragmatic.[19]

Reed Dickerson, on the other hand, did not attempt to classify or assign labels to the different approaches to statutory construction. Instead, he wrote in terms of basic concepts, listing seven of them from the ascertainment of meaning to the statute and its context.[20]

As can be seen from this summary, it is very easy to become bogged down in classifying and labeling the different approaches to statutory construction. There is no agreement among scholars on either the classifications or the labels. New approaches keep developing, particularly as statutory construction receives more attention from academics. As Judge Posner has commented, statutory construction scholarship has become "cacophonous."[21]

Professor Martineau has developed an explanation of statutory construction that rejects the use of theoretical approaches to explain how courts construe statutes. Building on the work of Karl Llewellyn and his own work and scholarship in the field of the appellate process, he concluded that judges do not use theories of statutory construction to reach a result in a case involving the text of a statute. Instead, they use one or more of the theories to explain or rationalize a decision reached on other grounds.[22] From the standpoint of the legislative drafter, knowing how different approaches to statutory construction are classified is not so important as knowing that sometimes a court will limit its search for meaning to the words of the statute, and sometimes it will go beyond the words. When the search is limited to the words, the drafter must know the conventions and guidelines that are available for the court to support or reject a particular meaning. The drafter must also know what will prompt a court to go outside the text of the statute, and what the courts will look at when they do. These topics are covered in the rest of this chapter.

E. INTERNAL AIDS TO CONSTRUCTION

Over the years, the courts have developed a whole range of rules or canons that they use to justify their construction of particular statutes. Most of these canons concern the use of language. There are three important things to understand about the canons. First, they are not inflexible rules but merely conventions of writing or rebuttable presumptions. This means they can be followed or ignored at will. Second, when used their function is not to compel a result but to justify a result reached for other reasons. They are applied after the fact to support a construction adopted for reasons the court may or may not reveal in its opinion. Third, notwithstanding almost universal criticism of the canons by academics and thoughtful judges, the courts continue to use them as though they are the bases on which statutes are construed. The best known criticism of the canons is that of Karl Llewellyn who demonstrated that for almost every canon there is another canon that will support the opposite conclusion.[23] Judge Posner has gone further and suggested that some of the best known canons or their premises are simply wrong.[24] Professor Cass Sunstein, however, argues that Llewellyn's criticism were overstated and that the canons do influence judicial behavior "insofar as they reflected background norms" that help to give meaning to words in the statute or resolve hard cases. He further states that the use of general guides to construction can be found in every area of the law.[25]

Among the most commonly used canons are the following:

a) The mention of one thing excludes another (*"expressio unius est exelusius alterius"*).

b) A word takes some of its meaning from the words with which it is used (*"noscitur a sociis"*).

c) A general word is limited by the more specific words with which it is used (*"ejusdem generis"*).

d) Words are used in their ordinary meaning unless a technical meaning is suggested by the other words in the statute.

e) Every word in a statute must be given effect.

f) Different words have different meanings.

g) Words are to be interpreted according to the rules of grammar and punctuation.

h) The same word used in different places has the same meaning.

i) "Shall" is mandatory and "may" is permissive.

j) "And" is conjunctive and "or" is disjunctive.

The positive side of these canons for the drafter is that in most instances they simply represent principles of good writing. The wise drafter will use them both because they aid in good writing and because the courts usually presume the drafter will follow them. The negative side, of course, is a court can ignore them whenever they do not lead to the construction the court wants to adopt.

F. WHEN THE COURTS USE EXTERNAL SOURCES

The best place to start is with the rule concerning when a court will not go outside the text of a statute before addressing when it will do so. This is the so called plain meaning rule. That rule was expressed by the United States Supreme Court in the following terms: "When the language is plain and admits of no more than one meaning, the duty of interpretation does not arise, and the rules which are said to aid doubtful meanings need no discussion."[26] It can thus be seen that the rule as to external sources is a corollary of the plain meaning rule. Under that rule, a court interpreting a statute will attempt to decide what it means by considering first only its words. Only if that process fails to provide an answer to the question of meaning does the court go outside the "four corners" of the statute.

As might be expected, a rule so simple to state is far more difficult to put into practice. The first problem is inherent in attempting to ascertain the meaning of any word. As Justice Frankfurter once said, words are "symbols of meaning."[27] They can be ambiguous, vague, general, or precise. Further, words when used in a statute (or any writing) do not stand in isolation. They have a context, and that context helps to give meaning to the words.[28] This leads many to argue that one can never construe the words in a statute by looking only at the words but always must refer to external sources before arriving at a particular meaning. Under this analysis, the plain meaning rule defies reality.

Another problem is whether, when a word or clause in a statute appears on the surface to have a plain meaning, a court can consult external sources to establish that the meaning is not plain, thus allowing resort to the same or other external sources to resolve the question of meaning. Strict advocates of the plain meaning rule refuse to admit this initial consultation is proper, considering it a trap that will permit resort to external sources in every case, thereby eliminating the plain meaning rule. Of course, those who think the plain meaning rule is nonsense to begin with have no difficulty, consulting external sources at any step in the construction process.

The courts in between the two ends of the spectrum cause the most difficulty. They sometimes will construe a statute without going outside of its words, with or without citing the plain meaning rule in support of their conclusions. In other cases, the courts will rely on external sources both to demonstrate that the meaning of the statute is unclear and to resolve the uncertainty. Does this mean the courts are being inconsistent? Not if the way courts use the techniques of statutory construction is understood. These techniques, including the plain meaning rule and the canons of construction, should not be viewed as the means by which a court reaches a conclusion as to the meaning of a statute. They are, rather, the means by which the court justifies its conclusion as to the appropriate construction of the statute in light of what it sees as the equities of the case and the needs of society. A lack of understanding of this fact is what leads many persons to think that when a court uses one technique or canon rather than another, it is acting improperly. This applies to the plain meaning rule as well as to others. If the plain meaning rule provides the result the court thinks is appropriate in the case, it will use it. If not, it will go outside of the words of the statute to external sources, without regard to whether the external sources provide the basis for going external or for reaching the construction the court thinks is proper.

G.　EXTERNAL SOURCES[29]

A court will refer to external sources for two principal purposes—to ascertain the general purpose of the statute and to aid in construing a particular provision. A list of external sources a court will consult includes:

1) the title, purpose clause, and section headings in the statute;

2) legislative history including committee reports, floor debates, statements of sponsors, statements of drafters, committee hearings, analyses by legislative counsel, amendments accepted or rejected at any stage, reports of drafting bodies, actions and discussions of prior, contemporaneous, or subsequent proposed or adopted legislation, statements by the executive concerning the bill, related judicial and administrative decisions, and facts of which the courts will take judicial notice;

3) related statutes;

4) similar statutes in other jurisdictions and judicial constructions of them;

5) administrative constructions.

Some of these references have their own canons of construction. They include the following:

1) a statute will be construed in accordance with its purpose;

2) a remedial statute will be construed liberally;

3) a statute in derogation of the common law will be construed strictly;

4) statutes "in *pari materia*" must be construed together;

5) when a statute was previously adopted and construed in another state, that construction will be followed;

6) definitions and rules of construction in an interpretation statute will be followed;

7) titles, purpose clauses, and section headings are not controlling but may be used as guides to meaning;

8) words and phrases that received judicial construction before enactment are to receive the same construction;

9) constructions of an administrative agency charged with administering the statute are to be followed unless clearly erroneous.

Once again, because there is a counter canon to almost every canon,[30] the drafter should look at these canons only as rationales for decisions construing statutes, not as rules that determine the meaning of a word or phrase or its application in the case.

Of the external sources, the two that cause the most debate are legislative history and administrative interpretations of a statute. Many decisions of the United States Supreme Court are supported by majority opinions citing to legislative history and opposed by minority opinions citing the same or different legislative history. In many respects citing legislative history is like citing to the canons of statutory construction— you can usually find in the history something to support or oppose a particular construction of a statute, just as you can usually find a canon to support one construction and another canon to support a different construction.[31] The result has been a revival of the argument against the validity of the use of any legislative history to find meaning beyond the words of the statute. Justice Scalia has been the most prominent and articulate advocate of this position.[32]

Another debate has been over the extent to which courts should rely on the construction of a statute by the agency charged with administering it. So long as the rule was that the administration agency's construction was to be given some but not binding weight there was little difficulty. When the Supreme Court held in the Chevron[33] case, however, that the agency's construction was to be followed unless it was unreasonable or contrary to a specific intent of Congress, some observers thought the court went too far in giving deference and abdicated judicial responsibility.[34] Several subsequent decisions of the Supreme Court suggest the court may have withdrawn somewhat from the position adopted in Chevron.[35]

In summary, what a court will do when faced with a statutory construction problem can seldom be predicted with certainty in advance of its decision. This chapter is designed to make the legislative drafter aware of the uncertainties of statutory construction in the courts and in particular the techniques the courts can use to justify the construction it adopts, following the maxim that to be forewarned is to be forearmed. The purpose of this book, and of chapters 5–9 in particular, is to provide the drafter with the tools to limit, insofar as is humanly possible, the opportunities for courts to engage in statutory construction to reach a result not intended by the proponent of the statute. This may be difficult, but to the extent that a statute's proponent has an intent, the drafter should make it known to the court and the court should follow it in construing the statute.

Endnotes

1. For further detail on the final judgment rule see R. Martineau, Modern Appellate Practice: Federal and State Civil Appeals sec. 4.1–4.9 (1983).

2. Catlin v. United States, 324 U.S. 229, 233, 65 S.Ct. 631, 633 (1945).

3. Forgay v. Conrad, 47 U.S. (6 How.) 201, 202 (1848). See also Redish, The Pragmatic Approach to Appealability in the Federal Courts, 75 Columbia L. Rev. 89 (1975).

4. Coopers & Lybrand v. Livesay, 437 U.S. 463, 98 S.Ct. 2454 (1978); Cohen v. Beneficial Industrial Loan Corp., 337 U.S. 541, 69 S.Ct. 1221 (1949).

5. Coopers & Lybrand v. Livesay, note 4, supra.

6. Mitchell v. Forsyth, 472 U.S. 511, 105 S.Ct. 2806 (1985).

7. R. Dickerson, The Interpretation and Application of Statutes 13–33 (1975).

8. W. Eskridge, Jr. and P. Frickey, Cases and Materials on Legislation Ch. 7 (3rd ed. 2000).

9. The author's distinction between interpretation and application is also made in de Sloovere, The Function of Judge and Jury in the Interpretation of Statutes, 46 Harvard L. Rev. 1086, 1095 (1933).

10. 2A Sutherland, Statutes and Statutory Construction § 45.05 (4th ed. rev., 1984). "For the interpretation of statutes, intent of the legislature is the criterion most often recited. An overwhelming majority of judicial opinions considering statutory issues are written in the context of legislative intent." In the footnote to the text there is a citation to a case from almost every jurisdiction.

11. Radin, Statutory Interpretation, 43 Harvard L. Rev. 863 (1930).

12. This view is set forth in H. Hart and L. Sacks, The Legal Process (Tent. ed. 1958). See the discussion of the Hart and Sacks approach in W. Eskridge, Jr. and P. Frickey, Legislation 575–77 (1988).

13. R. Dickerson, supra note 7 at 229–33.

14. C. Ogden & I. Richards, The Meaning of Meaning (10th ed. 1959); Williams, Language and the Law, 61 Law Q. Rev. 384, 392 (1945).

15. Riggs v. Palmer, 115 N.Y. 506, 22 N.E. 188 (1889).

16. Commonwealth v. Maxwell, 271 Pa. 378, 114 A. 825 (1921). Contra, People ex rel. Fyfe v. Barnett, 319 Ill. 403, 150 N.E. 290 (1925).

17. W. Eskridge, Jr. and P. Frickey, supra note 8 at 571–72. In a more recent law review article, Eskridge and Frickey divide the approaches to statutory construction into three. The first emphasizes legislative intent, the second legislative purpose, and the third text. They argue that all three fail to establish an overriding and objective foundation for interpreting legislation and have three common weaknesses. Each rests on questionable premis-

es about the nature of interpretation and the legislative process. None can systematically produce determinate results in hard cases and thus cannot claim to be objective. Finally, none persuades that its underlying values are so important as to include the others. They argue that any grand theory of statutory construction has a basic weakness in its emphasis on the general over the particular and that statutory construction works in different ways in different cases.

They then propose their own grand theory which they call "practical reasoning." Using the U.S. supreme court as a model, they argue that the court "considers a broad range of textual, historical, and evaluative evidence when it enters statutes. In the easy cases, most of the evidence points in the same direction and is thereby mutually reinforcing. In the hard cases, however, the evidence points in different directions, and the court critically analyzes each textual or historical or evaluative argument, both as to its own cogency and as to its cogency and light of the other evidence." Eskridge and Frickey, Statutory Interpretation as Practical Reasoning, 42 Stanford L. Rev. 321, 322–23 (1990).

18. Schanck, The Only Game in Town: Contemporary Interpretative Theory, Statutory Construction, and Legislative Histories, 82 Law Library J. 419, 421 (1990).

19. Posner, Legislation and Its Interpretation: A Primer, 68 Nebraska L. Rev. 431–434 (1989).

20. R. Dickerson, The Interpretation and Application of Statutes 13–136 (1975).

21. Posner, supra note 19 at 434.

22. Martineau, Craft and Technique, Not Canons and Grand Theories: A Neo–Realist View of Statutory Construction, 62 George Washington L. Rev. 1 (1993).

23. Llewellyn, 3 Vanderbilt L. Rev. 395, 401–06 (1950), reprinted in K. Llewellyn, The Common Law Tradition 521–35 (1960). For a more recent appraisal, see Manning, Legal Realism and the Canons, 5 Green Bag 2d 283 (2002).

24. Posner, Statutory Interpretation—in the Classroom and in the Courtroom, 50 U. of Chicago L. Rev. 800, 806 (1983).

25. Sunstein, Interpreting Statutes in the Regulatory State, 103 Harvard L. Rev. 407, 452–53 (1989). For a debate on the Sunstein position see Moglen and Pierce, Sunstein's New Canons: Choosing the Fictions of Statutory Interpretation, 57 U. of Chicago L. Rev. 1203 (1990) and Sunstein, Principles, Not Fictions, 57 U. of Chicago L. Rev. 1247 (1990).

26. Caminetti v. United States, 242 U.S. 470, 485, 37 S.Ct. 192, 194 (1917).

27. Frankfurter, Some Reflections on the Readings of Statutes, 47 Columbia L. Rev. 527, 528 (1947).

28. Id at 533.

29. For a more complete discussion of courts use of external sources, see W. Eskridge, Jr. and P. Frickey, supra note 8 at ch. 7.

30. Llewellyn, supra note 23. For a more recent appraisal, see Manning, Legal Realism and the Canons, 5 Green Bag 2d 283 (2002).

31. Judge Abner Mikva quotes Harold Leventhal, his colleague in the U.S. Court of Appeals for the D.C. Circuit, as saying that "one can always find some friends in the legislative history." Mikva, Statutory Interpretation: Getting the Law to be Less Common, 50 Ohio State L.J. 979, 982 (1989).

32. Justice Antonin Scalia of the U.S. supreme court has been particularly vocal in his criticism of courts relying on legislative history. See Wald, The Sizzling Sleeper: The Use of Legislative History in Construing Statutes in the 1988–89 Term of the United States Supreme Court, 39 The American U. L. Rev. 277, 281–86 (1990). For the views of another member of the supreme court, made before he was on the court, see Breyer, On the Uses of Legislative History in Interpreting Statutes, 65 S. Cal. L. Rev. 845 (1992).

33. Chevron U.S.A., Inc. v. Natural Resources Defense Council, Inc., 467 U.S. 837, 104 S.Ct. 2778 (1984).

34. Pierce, Chevron and its Aftermath: Judicial Review of Agency Interpretations of Statutory Provisions, 41 Vanderbilt L. Rev. 301 (1988); Starr, Sunstein, Willard, Morrison & Levin, Judicial Review of Administrative Action in a Conservative Era, 39 Administrative L. Rev. 353 (1987).

35. Pierce, supra note 33 at 303, note 15.

Chapter 13

ORGANIZATION AND SUBDIVISION OF A BILL

A. INTRODUCTION

This chapter examines the organization and subdivision of a typical bill. It shows the order in which the various parts of a bill are arranged and discusses the content of each part and whether the part is required or optional. It also shows how to assign numbers and letters to each subdivision.

B. ARRANGEMENT

1. Identifying Prefix and Number

a. Federal

When a bill or joint resolution is introduced, custom dictates that it be identified with a combination of letters and numbers. A bill receives the letters *"H.R."* if introduced in the House of Representatives or *"S."* in the Senate, followed by the number given to it. Numbers are assigned consecutively in the order introduced. Thus, the 156th bill introduced in the House in a particular congress is marked *"H.R. 156"* and in the Senate *"S. 156."* The number is usually not known in advance so the drafter merely puts the *"H.R."* or *"S."* at the top of the first page, leaving a space for the number to be added when the bill is introduced. The same system applies to a joint resolution except that the title designation is *"H.J.R."* or *"S.J.R."*

b. State

States differ widely on the prefix used along with numbers to identify a bill. In Ohio for example, a bill introduced in the house of representatives is designated *"H.B."* and the senate *"S.B."* followed by the number assigned in the order introduced. In Wisconsin, instead of initials the year and the name of the house are used, e.g., *"1990 Assembly Bill"* or *"1990 Senate Bill."* These designations vary from state to state. Custom rather than express provision in a constitution, statute, or rule usually determines the proper designation. If the drafter does not put the appropriate designation on the bill, a legislative official will do so at the time of introduction.

2. Designation

As discussed in chapter 13, section C 1, the next item to appear is the designation *"A Bill"* or its alternative as determined by local rule or custom.

3. Title

Immediately following the words *"A Bill"* but not on the same line is the title, constitutionally required in most states. The title begins with the words *"to"* or *"relating to"* and then gives the general purpose of the bill. As noted in chapter 14, section C 2, the title should be general rather than specific. It should not be long. Some states also require a reference to the code sections affected by the bill.

4. Enacting Clause

As noted in chapter 13, sections 13 B (federal) and 13 C 3 (state), an enacting clause in the precise terms set forth in a constitution or statute is required for both federal and state legislation.

5. Short Title

It is common in lengthy federal legislation but not in state legislation for the first section of a bill to provide a short title by which the bill when enacted may be cited. A typical provision is *"Sec 1. This act may be cited as the Voting Rights Act of 1990."* A short title is advisable only if the entire act will be incorporated into a single place in the code and not divided up among a number of separate chapters or sections of the code. By its terms the section does not require the use of the short title. By the same token, its absence does not prevent an act from being called by short title, as is the case with the Judiciary Act of 1789.

6. Statement of Purpose, Policy, or Findings

Another preliminary section found in some federal legislation but seldom in state legislation is a section in which the legislative body expresses in general terms the purpose of the bill or the policy that underlies it, or makes findings that provide the factual basis for the enactment of the bill. These statements are useful to a court construing legislation to the extent that a court is willing to look at something other than the plain meaning of the words being construed. These statements are dangerous to the extent that a proponent or drafter thinks that a statement can be a substitute for clarity of expression. Courts can rely on them or not, depending not only upon the court's willingness to consider context but also upon whether the statement supports or is contrary to the construction the court favors, as discussed in chapter 11.

7.   Section that Adds, Amends, Repeals, Reenacts

The part of the bill that contains its substantive provisions must begin with language that puts the provisions into the jurisdiction's code as an amendment to it. This is usually placed in section 1 unless there are preceding sections that include a short title or statement of purpose, policy or findings.

The amendment can be accomplished in several ways, depending upon local custom. One is to enact a new section. Another is to provide that an existing section is amended by either adding new language to the section or by striking out existing language and inserting new language in its place. Another is to repeal the section being amended and then reenact the section with the new language in its place. The simplest way to ascertain the precise language used in the jurisdiction for which the drafter is preparing a bill is to look in the jurisdiction's compilation of recently enacted legislation. They are called the *"United States Statutes at Large"* for federal laws. In the states they have various titles such as *"session laws"* or *"public laws."*

Many states require that the entire section being amended be included in this part of the bill. The language being deleted must be shown in some distinctive way such as striking through the deleted words with the new language shown in all capital letters, e.g., *"the tax on income is ~~seven (7)~~ EIGHT (8) percent."* Alternatives are to put the deleted language in brackets or to underscore new language. For arrangement of the substantive provisions, see chapter 12, section C.

8.   Repeal Section

Local custom may require that after the section of the bill that provides for the amendment to the code there be another section that repeals the language currently in the code. Technically, this repeal section should not be necessary because the amending section accomplishes the change in the law and the old section is no longer in effect. Nonetheless, if local custom requires a repealing section, the drafter should include it.

9.   Substantive Provision

See chapter 12, section C.

10.   Emergency or Urgency Clause

In some jurisdictions, in order for legislation to go into effect immediately rather than at a later date specified in the constitution, the bill must specify in its title that it is an emergency or urgency bill and then include a section that states the reasons why the bill must go into effect immediately. Usually emergency or urgency legislation must be passed by a super majority of each house of the legislature. The courts usually accept without question a legislative determination that an emergency or urgency exists.

11. Severability Section

A traditional provision in a bill is a severability clause, usually contained in a separate section. This clause specifies that if a provision of the act is declared invalid, the rest of the act remains in effect unless it cannot be made effective without the invalid provision. This type of provision is not necessary because the courts uniformly construe laws in this way with or without a severability clause. In addition, many general interpretation statutes have a severability clause. It is only confusing to the courts to put a severability clause in some bills but not in others. If, however, the proponent wants all or part of a bill to fail if a provision in the bill is declared invalid, then the bill should have a clause that expressly identifies the provision that may be held invalid and the provision that is to be ineffective in that event. For example, a bill may establish a program and impose a tax to pay for it. The proponent or the legislature may conclude that it does not want to fund the program from any other source and would prefer the program to fail if the special tax is declared invalid. In that case, the bill should contain a separate section that so provides.

12. Saving Section

A court will usually construe an act to be applicable to a legal relationship previously established, conduct that has occurred and for which a penalty is provided, or a proceeding begun before the act is effective. To avoid this result, a general interpretation statute will often include a general saving section that provides just the opposite, absent express language in the act. If there is no general interpretation statute, a specific saving section will be necessary to prevent application of the act to existing relationships or proceedings or past conduct. If there is a general saving section but the proponent wants the bill to affect existing relationships or proceedings or past conduct, then the drafter should include a clause to achieve that result.

13. Temporary or Implementing Provisions

On many occasions the provisions of a bill will require a phasing in or implementation before the bill can be fully effective. For example, a bill that creates a board or commission of nine members each with three year terms and provides that the terms of three members expire each year cannot begin with nine members each of whom has a three year term. To avoid this problem, the bill should provide that when the first members are appointed, three members are to be appointed for initial terms of one year, three with initial terms of two years, and three with terms of three years. It is not necessary or wise to include the provisions relating to the initial terms in the permanent provisions that will be included in the code because they will affect only the first members. Rather than cluttering up the code with provisions that have only temporary effect, the technique used is to put the initial term provisions in a separate section that is included in the enacted bill and the session laws, but not in the code.

14. Effective Date

A constitutional provision or general statute will usually provide that every act is effective on a uniform date. The date may be immediately upon or a specific number of days after approval by the executive or some other event. If there is a general effective date, the bill need not have a section that establishes an effective date. If, however, there is no general provision, or if the general provision allows an act to establish a different effective date and the proponent wants a different date, then a drafter must include an effective date section. A typical provision would read: *"Section 4. This act takes effect immediately (or 30 days after approval by the governor)."*

C. ORGANIZATION OF SUBSTANTIVE PROVISIONS

The heart of any legislation is, of course, its substantive provisions. Of the remaining 13 portions of a bill listed in chapter 12, section B, most are necessary in every bill while a few are required only in certain circumstances. None of them, however, actually makes a change in the rights, duties, powers, or status of a public or private person or entity. Thus none of them is the direct focus of attention when a court is called upon to construe a statute. The bill drafter is also primarily concerned with the substantive provisions because they are the means for translating the ideas of the proponent into language that will accomplish the goals of the proponent. To aid the drafter in achieving that end, chapters 5–9 set forth principles on writing style and related topics.

Another aspect of drafting that can affect readability and understandability is the organization of the substantive provisions. Just as organization is important to a sentence, paragraph, chapter, or other form of writing, so is it equally important in legislative or rule drafting. Before beginning to draft, the drafter should consider the principal divisions of the substantive portion of the legislation, decide how best to arrange them, and then consider the arrangement of the principal divisions.

There are four principal divisions of the substantive portion of legislation—definitions, public, administration, and sanction or remedy.

1. Definitions

Definitions are discussed in chapter 8, section I. As explained there, not every bill or rule requires a definition section. If there is one, however, the drafter should place it at the beginning of the substantive provisions. If a definition is applicable to only one of several sections, then the proper place for the definition is at the beginning of that section.

2. Public

After the definitions, the next provisions to place in the legislation or rule are those that affect the public. In this context *"public"* means the class of persons or entities that is the object of the legislation. The provisions may be generally applicable to everyone such as a criminal statute, or to some special class such as employers, corporations, nurses, government employees, teachers, law enforcement officers, judges, municipal corporations, schools, day care providers, or any other class or subdivision of a class that the legislative mind may consider worthy of special legislative treatment. It is in these sections that rights and privileges are created, status declared, or duties and responsibilities imposed.

Within this portion of the legislation, it is ordinarily best to start with the general provisions, and then move to the particular. The latter should include special subclassifications, exceptions, qualifiers, or other provision that limits the applicability of the general provisions.

Most legislation affects some portion of the public and thus has this type of provision. The only exceptions are those that are concerned solely with administration or a sanction or remedy for a violation of provisions affecting the public previously enacted.

3. Administration

Much if not most legislation is self executing in the sense that it is effective by the fact of its enactment. If the power of government is needed to enforce some provision of the legislation, the enforcement occurs as a result of action of law enforcement officers in the case of criminal statutes or the courts in the case of both criminal and civil statutes. As is generally known, however, much legislation requires the action of one or more governmental entities or officers to administer and enforce its provisions. The establishment of these entities or officers and the granting of their powers and duties will normally follow the public provisions, but may also precede them if considered more significant. Common subjects covered are the agency's organization, personnel, and powers, in that order.

For recommended language for creating an entity or officer, see chapter 8, section L.

4. Sanction or Remedy

The last substantive division includes the sanction or remedy for a violation of one of the public provisions. The sanction or remedy can be civil or criminal and can be imposed by a court or governmental entity or official. If monetary, the sanction can be payable to a private party, governmental entity or officer, or court. A law does not have to provide expressly for a sanction, either because it is not legally enforceable or because it is enforceable through some preexisting legal mechanism.

The proper way to establish a criminal penalty is set out in chapter 8, section K.

D. SYSTEM OF SUBDIVISION

When drafting legislation or a rule, the drafter must organize it with a system of subdivision including a system of identification of each subdivision. In subdividing, the drafter is not free to choose the system of subdivision the drafter thinks most appropriate. Except in the rarest of circumstances, the legislative or rule making body will have previously enacted or adopted legislation or rules that will have been subdivided according to a particular system. The drafter should always follow that system. Otherwise the integration of the new legislation or rule into those previously enacted or adopted will be virtually impossible. Before putting the first word to paper or in the computer, the drafter must review the existing legislation or rules and follow the subdivision system found in them.

Just looking at the compilations of previous legislation or rules found in codes or rule books is not sufficient. The drafter must also look at the documents that preceded the compilation. For legislation there will be a bill or ordinance as it was originally introduced, the act or ordinance as it was enacted by the legislative body, and the substantive provisions of the act or ordinance as they were incorporated into a code. A rule will usually be preceded first by a proposed rule as it was submitted to the rule making body for its consideration or published by it for comment and second by the rule as incorporated into an order of the rulemaking body adopting the rule. The substantive provisions of the rule may then be incorporated into a compilation of rules.

For the drafter, the most important document is the bill as introduced in the legislative body or the proposed rule as submitted to the rulemaking body or published by it for comment. These documents are always available, but may not be easily accessible to the drafter who is not an employee of the legislative or rule making body or accustomed to dealing with it. A good law library should have copies of bills introduced in the U.S. Congress and the legislatures for the state in which it is located. Proposed federal agency rules can be found in the Federal Register and state rules in comparable state publications. Not all states have registers. If a state does not, the drafter may have to contact the agency and ask for a sample proposed rule.

Court rules are even more problematic. For a state supreme court, proposed rules may be published in a bar publication or in the advance sheets for court opinions. Adopted rules are usually included in the bound volumes of the opinions of the court and included in compilations of court rules. Local court rules are difficult to locate in any form. Proposed federal court rules of the type adopted by the U.S. Supreme Court are published in the advance sheets for the Supreme Court Reporter, Federal Reporter, Federal Supplement, and Federal Rules Decisions, as are the rules when adopted. Circuit rules of the federal courts of appeals are published when adopted in the advance sheets of the Federal Reporter and included in a separate volume of Title 28 of the U.S. Code Annotated but are often not published in proposal form.

Local rules adopted by the federal district courts are not published and are available only from the court or, in a few instances, from local bar associations or local publishers.

Local legislation adopted by counties or municipal corporations is very difficult to find except in those with large populations. Rules adopted by local administrative agencies can seldom be obtained except from the agencies and almost never in compiled form. In every case, the burden is on the drafter to take whatever steps are necessary to ascertain the proper organization for the item to be drafted and to follow it.

The most common subdivision system alternates between letters and numbers, and, as to letters, between upper and lower case, as shown in the following example.

1.

2.

(a)

(b)

    (1)

    (2)

        (A)

        (B)

            (i)

            (ii)

The drafter should, of course, follow the subdivision system in the code or other compilation into which the bill will be incorporated when enacted.

Chapter 14

FORMAL REQUIREMENTS
AND LIMITATIONS

A. INTRODUCTION

Formal requirements and limitations affecting legislation at the federal and state levels are of three types. One type goes to the form or style of the proposed legislation, the second to its content, and the third to the process by which the proposal moves from introduction to enactment. In chapter 10 the legislative process is described. The chapter does not indicate whether various steps in the process are required or mere custom, and of those required, whether the requirement is contained in a constitution, statute, or legislative rule. There is also no discussion of whether the failure to follow a requirement invalidates the legislation. The reason those two topics are left out is a result of the nature of this book, which is concerned with the drafting of legislation rather than the process by which a proposal once introduced as a bill becomes law. The purpose of chapter 10 is to give the drafter only sufficient information to perform the drafting task.

This chapter is concerned with the first two types of requirements and limitations, those that affect the form or style of the proposed legislation, and those that affect its content. Both directly affect the drafter because they control to some degree what the drafter must or may not include in the proposed legislation.

The formal requirements and limitations can be found in three places—constitution, statutes, and rules of legislative bodies. In addition, custom dictates some working practices, but these do not rise to the level of formal requirements.

A major difference exists between federal and state law as to where the requirements and limitations are found. Those that affect federal legislation are statutory only. Neither the constitution nor the rules of the senate and house of representatives contain requirements or limitations other than the limitations on the powers of the federal government. In the states, on the other hand, most of the requirements are found in their constitutions or legislative rules but only a few in statutes. Where a requirement is located may affect whether a court will hold a statute invalid because of a violation of one of the requirements or limitations. The drafter, however, should treat all of the requirements and limitations as equally important and comply with each of them. The goal of the drafter should be to keep to a minimum not only the occasions on which a court can construe legislation contrary to the intent of the proponent but also those on which it can find legislation invalid for improper form or content.

B.   FEDERAL

Four types of federal legislative documents exist—a bill, joint resolution, concurrent resolution, and simple resolution. Federal statutory law can be made by the enactment of a bill or a joint resolution. A bill can amend a law originally enacted by a joint resolution, and a joint resolution can amend a law originally enacted by a bill. The equal status of a bill and a joint resolution results from the fact that the federal constitution provides the same procedures for the enactment of each, including presentment to the president for approval or veto. A concurrent resolution, on the other hand, usually deals with the operation of the two houses of Congress or expresses facts, principles, opinions, or purposes of the two houses. A simple resolution covers the same areas but for only one house.[1] This section is concerned only with bills and joint resolutions.

All of the requirements and limitations are found in sections 101–105 of title 1 of the U.S. Code. The only item required by these sections to be included is an enactment clause for a bill and a resolving clause for a joint resolution. The language of these clauses is specified by sections 101 and 102. For a bill it is "Be it enacted by the Senate and House of Representatives of the United States of America in Congress assembled." For a joint resolution the language is "Resolved by the Senate and House of Representatives of the United States of America in Congress assembled." Section 105 specifies a specific style and title for legislation making an appropriation.

The sections impose only two limitations on the form of a bill or joint resolution. Section 103 prohibits an enacting or resolving clause after the first section while section 104 requires that each section be numbered and "as nearly as may be" contain a single proposition of enactment.

C.   STATE

For reasons that can best be described as historical, states impose substantially greater requirements and limitations as to form or style and content than does federal law.

The requirements and limitations can be grouped as follows:

1. Designation

Most states require that any formal proposal for the legislature to enact a law be done by a bill. In some states the constitution expressly states that no law may be enacted except by bill, as in article III, section 15 of the Ohio constitution. In others, the constitution merely makes reference to "bill" in setting forth the requirements on enactment of laws. For these reasons a proposal introduced in the legislature is designated "A Bill" or some variation of that term. In Minnesota, for example, the designation is "A Bill for an Act." Whatever the requirement, it is essential for the drafter to find out what it is and to comply with it.

2. Title

Almost every state constitution requires a bill to have a title.[2] The requirement is usually tied to the single subject requirement, discussed in chapter 13, section C 4. California is typical in its article IV, section 9: "A statute shall embrace but one subject, which shall be expressed in its title." Ohio is even more demanding, insisting in article 11, section 15(D) that the subject be "clearly" expressed in its title. The major risk in drafting a title is to make it underinclusive.[3] This usually results from putting too much detail in the title. In an effort to be specific as to what is in a bill, a drafter may be tempted to include substantial detail. The problem created by this effort is that if some portion of it is not mentioned, some or all of the bill may be invalid. This problem can often result from an amendment made after the bill is introduced but without an amendment to the title. The better strategy is to be very general. Instead of having the title read, "*A Bill to increase the maximum rate of the tax on income from seven to eight per cent*," the title should read, "*A Bill relating to the tax on income*." It is customary in some states that the code sections affected by the bill be set out in the title.

3. Enacting Clause

Just as important as the title to the validity of a bill is the enacting clause. Almost every state constitution requires that for a bill to become a law it must have an enacting clause.[4] Not only is an enacting clause required, but these constitutions specify the exact words of the enacting clause.[5] Inclusion of the precise words specified is absolutely essential for the drafter. Some examples are Ohio, which requires "Be it enacted by the general assembly of the state of Ohio," while Michigan's is "The People of the State of Michigan enact." Some variation might be permitted in the order of the words, but unless some form of the word "*enact*" appears, a court will likely hold the statute invalid.

4. Single Subject

As noted in chapter 13, section C 3, constitutional requirements for a title are usually joined with a prohibition against a bill containing more than a single subject.[6] Courts are usually very reluctant to use it to strike down legislation unless the court can find no logical relationship between the various subjects contained in the bill. One simple test is framing the title. If the drafter has difficulty in framing a general title that fairly encompasses the subjects in the bill, the drafter should consult with the bill's proponent whether to drop out one of the subjects or to draft a separate bill for each subject.

5. Text of Amended Statute

Some constitutions provide that an existing statute may not be amended unless the new act contains the full text of the amended statute.[7] This means that the bill must repeal the section of the statute being amended and then enact the old section with the amendment setting out the entire text as amended in the bill. The bill cannot simply contain the new words to be added to the existing text. Most legislative rules go further and require that the bill indicate the words being repealed by a line drawn through them and the words being added in capital letters or some other style that identifies the old language being repealed and the new language being substituted or added.

6. Other Restrictions on Content

State constitutions as well as the federal constitution impose a wide variety of restrictions on the content of statutes, from requiring that a statute have a public purpose to prohibiting bills of attainder or interferences with freedom of the press or religion. They include debt limits, prohibitions on special rather than general laws, and restrictions on internal improvements or loaning of the state's credit. The drafter should be generally aware of these, and point out to the proponent a blatant constitutional violation. The drafter, however, is usually not expected to be the constitutional law adviser to the proponent.

D. LOCAL LEGISLATION

While state constitutions usually give substantial attention to state legislation, they seldom mention local legislation adopted by counties, cities, towns, or other authorized forms of municipal government, all of which are referred to as ordinances. The major exception is when municipal home rule is granted. Requirements as to form are found, if at all, only in state legislation or municipal charters. At most, ordinances are required to have a title and an enacting or ordaining clause, and usually only the latter is absolutely necessary.[8]

The proper designation of an enactment as an ordinance or as a resolution is not always clear. Usually, an ordinance is required for a continuing rule or restriction that is legislative in character. A resolution, on the other hand, deals with expressions of opinion, temporary matters, or administrative detail of a ministerial nature.[9]

Endnotes

1. E. Willett, Jr., How Our Laws Are Made 5–7 (House Document 101–139, 1990).

2. 1A Sutherland, Statutes and Statutory Construction § 18.07 (4th ed. rev. 1984).

3. Id. at § 18.10.

4. Id. at § 19.01.

5. Id. at § 19.02. California recently eliminated its constitutional requirement for an enacting clause.

6. Id. at § 17.01.

7. Id. at § 22.16.

8. Id. at § 30.02; O. Reynolds, Jr., Local Government Law sec. 60 (1982).

9. Reynolds, supra note 9, at sec. 61.

*

Part V

DISTINCTIVE ASPECTS OF
DRAFTING ADMINISTRATIVE
AND COURT RULES

Chapter 15

ADMINISTRATIVE RULES*

A. INTRODUCTION

This chapter is to provide to the administrative rule drafter a basic understanding of the administrative rulemaking process and the limitations imposed upon it.

Drafting a rule differs from drafting legislation in that a legislature can address almost any issue it desires, while a rule maker is limited to the authority delegated to it by its enabling legislation. When drafting a rule, consequently, the drafter must always be aware of the scope of the authority delegated to the agency adopting the rule. If the legislature has granted broad discretion to an administrative agency, the agency has substantial leeway to exercise discretion and effect policy in the rule development process. If, however, the legislature has placed specific limitations on the agency's discretion, the freedom of the agency and thus of the rule drafter to make policy decisions through a rule is limited. The drafter of a rule must continually ask whether the rule is within the statutory authority of the agency and whether it is consistent with any prescriptive language in the statute.

Since the passage of the federal Administrative Procedure Act (APA)[1] in 1946, the growth of administrative rulemaking has been enormous. For example, the Code of Federal Regulations, which contains all administrative rules of the federal government, grew from 23,454 pages in 1948 to 144,177 pages in 2003. The Federal Register, in which most rules are initially proposed and promulgated, has grown from 15,505 pages in 1945 to 75,798 in 2003.

The growth in these publications is attributable both to the sheer volume of rules adopted by the agencies and departments of the federal government and to the constraints on the rulemaking process. No longer can an agency issue an entire set of rules with only a short page or two

* The author of this chapter is Robert J. Martineau, Jr., a member in the law firm of   Waller Lansden Dortch & Davis, PLLC, headquartered in Nashville, Tennessee.

description of the rule. Instead, lengthy preambles and other background documents supporting a rule evolved during the 1970's as key aspects of the rulemaking process. Procedural requirements such as the APA, other statutory mandates, less formal constraints such as executive orders, and judicial decisions have acted in concert to make the rulemaking process time consuming and cumbersome. Indeed, many agencies try to avoid the rulemaking process whenever possible through the use of informal adjudications, interpretative rules, or policy statements, which are not subject to the same procedural requirements as rules.[2]

Despite these efforts by agencies to avoid rulemaking, it remains a vital part of administrative law development today. The challenge to the rule drafter is to satisfy the various constraints on the process without sacrificing the goal of every rule to state with precision:

(1) Who may or may not do something, and

(2) What that person may or may not do.[3]

B. TYPES OF RULES AND RULEMAKING

The enactment of the APA in 1946 established the modern era in administrative law. The APA sets forth specific procedural requirements for all agencies to follow when issuing a rule. It defines a rule as

> the whole or part of an agency statement of general or particular applicability and future effect designed to implement, interpret, or prescribe law or policy or describing the organization, procedures, or practice.... [4]

The APA establishes three different classes of rules. The first is the rules not subject to a statutory requirement for public participation. The second is those rules governed by the informal rulemaking requirements of section 553 of the APA. This type of rulemaking is frequently referred to as notice and comment rulemaking. The third class is formal rules subject to the procedural requirements of sections 556 and 557. Calling section 553 rulemaking "informal" is somewhat of a misnomer, given the cumbersome nature of modern administrative law. It is still informal, however, in contrast to the formal trial-type procedures of sections 556 and 557.

The public participation requirements of the APA do not apply to interpretative rules, general statements of policy, or rules of agency organization, procedure, or practice.[5] An agency must, however, follow the formal (APA sections 556 and 557) or informal requirements (APA section 553) when adopting substantive rules. The Attorney General's Manual on the APA articulates the distinction between substantive (legislative) rules, interpretative rules, and statements of policy as follows:

> Substantive rules—rules, other than organizational or procedural ... issued by an agency pursuant to statutory authority and which

implement the statute.... Such rules have the force and effect of law.

Interpretative rules—rules or statements issued by an agency to advise the public of the agency's construction of the statutes and rules which it administers.

General statements of policy—statements issued by an agency to advise the public prospectively of the manner in which the agency proposes to exercise a discretionary power.[6]

Whether an agency action constitutes a rule subject to public participation requirements in its development is often in dispute and has been the subject of many judicial decisions. A rule drafter should proceed with extreme caution in determining whether a particular regulatory pronouncement should be drafted as a substantive rule, and thus subject to the procedural requirements for rules, or as an interpretive rule or general statement of policy and thus exempt from the procedural requirements. The U.S. Court of Appeals for the District of Columbia has said that a substantive rule is one that (1) has a present day binding effect, (2) grants rights and imposes obligations, and (3) leaves the agency and its decision makers little room to exercise discretion.[7] Thus, if it appears that a so-called policy statement is, in purpose or likely effect, one that narrowly limits administrative discretion, it will be taken for what it is—a binding rule of substantive law. If it is a binding rule, then it must be adopted under procedures that ensure public participation.

By far, most rules of federal agencies are adopted under the informal rulemaking process. Kenneth Davis characterizes informal rulemaking under section 553 of the APA as the most vital component of rulemaking because "it includes most substantive and legislative rules in furtherance of major governmental programs."[8] For this reason this chapter focuses on the requirements for informal rulemaking under the federal APA. Most states have some type of administrative procedure act establishing procedural requirements roughly paralleling those in the federal act. The state rule drafter should be aware of the state requirements.[9] In addition, states have a number of unique constitutional structures and other special factors that may affect a state rulemaking process. Those characteristics are discussed briefly in section C.

The third type of rulemaking, formal, is also known as trial-type rulemaking. This procedure is used infrequently by federal agencies. The requirements for formal rulemaking are similar to a civil trial and include procedural mechanisms such as the cross examination of witnesses. The procedure is used in licensing type proceedings or rulemakings for individual entities. It is are not typically used in legislative rulemaking.

C.   INITIATING THE RULEMAKING PROCESS

In most instances the agency itself initiates an effort to develop a rule, usually as a response to a statutory directive. Building consensus within an agency on how best to implement the statutory directive is often difficult and time consuming. Typically, a small group of agency staff with sufficient technical expertise to transform statutory language and a policy directive into a rule will do the initial drafting. The group will first compile the available factual and technical data. As it evaluates the data, it develops a set of options that can be supported by the data for the agency policy makers. Gradually, the group develops a consensus on the substance of a proposed rule. The next step is to expand the consensus throughout agency management and to seek the views of other interested agencies. In some instances, the agency will seek public comment before choosing one of the options. To obtain public comment some agencies give advance notice of proposed rulemaking or establish an advisory committee. The agency outlines what it is considering and solicits comments on alternatives.

Another mechanism agencies use with increased frequency is negotiated rulemaking, under which the agency convenes a meeting of representatives of various interest groups. By bringing major participants into the development of the rule prior to proposing a rule, the agency seeks to expedite the process, hear all viewpoints in a give-and-take forum, and limit potential challenges to the final rule.[10] In its 1990 session, Congress passed the Negotiated Rulemaking Act of 1990 establishing procedures for this process.[11] Negotiated rulemaking obviously affects the drafting process. To date, however, it has produced a relatively small number of rules.[12]

The rule drafter is usually faced with many competing policy concerns on how best to implement a statute. An agency is often afforded broad discretion by Congress in implementing a statute. In fact, even the decision to initiate a rulemaking effort is often a matter of discretion for an agency. Agencies are chronically faced with too few resources to pursue every regulatory effort they would like. The senior policy makers in an agency who have the authority to decide the areas in which the agency will adopt rules thus establish the priorities for the rule drafter.

The public also has an opportunity to influence an agency in making a decision to commence the rulemaking process. The APA provides in section 553(e) that an agency must afford "any interested person the right to petition for issuance, amendment, or repeal of a rule." Under the APA, a decision by an agency not to initiate rulemaking in response to a petition is judicially reviewable, but the standard of review is extremely narrow when the agency has discretion whether to act. Many statutes, however, provide a cause of action for a citizen if an agency fails to comply with a duty to act and some provide for more searching judicial review of an agency denial of a petition.[13] Through this type of mechanism, public interest groups and others are often able to affect the subject matter of an agency's rulemaking powers.

D. PROCEDURAL REQUIREMENTS FOR INFORMAL RULEMAKING

1. Federal APA Requirements

Section 553 of the APA prescribes the procedural requirements for informal rulemaking. As noted in section A 2, this requirement for notice and public participation does not apply to an interpretative rule, a general statement of policy, or a rule of agency practice and procedure. The agency must publish a notice of proposed rulemaking in the Federal Register specifying:

(1) a statement of the time, place, and nature of the public rulemaking proceedings;

(2) the legal authority under which the rule is proposed; and

(3) either the terms of substance of the proposed rule or a description of the subjects and issues involved.

The agency must subsequently provide interested persons the opportunity to participate in the process through submission of written data, views, or arguments, with or without the opportunity for oral presentations.

A statute may often contain additional procedural requirements applicable to rulemaking under the statute. These requirements may include a public hearing,[14] a response to significant comments,[15] a more detailed explanation of the rule in its preamble,[16] or more extensive record requirements.[17] A statute may also require that a rule be based on the substantial evidence standard rather than the rational basis or arbitrary and capricious standard.[18]

During the 1970's some courts, notably the U.S. Court of Appeals for the District of Columbia, attempted to require agencies to follow procedures beyond those in the APA or a specific underlying statute.[19] The Supreme Court, however, in Vermont Yankee Nuclear Power Corp. v. NRDC,[20] rejected that approach by stating that a court could not impose its own procedural requirements upon an agency beyond those required by section 553. Requirements to provide a clear and detailed statement of basis and purpose as well as to respond to significant comments, however, have survived Vermont Yankee because they are based on the language of section 553.

The agency must publish the final rule in the Federal Register. It must include in the rule a concise general statement of the basis and purpose of the rule. The final rule must also be a "logical outgrowth" of the proposed rule, that is the agency must have put the public on notice that the final rule is within the scope of the agency's original proposal.[21] The rule must also show compliance with other requirements such as the Paperwork Reduction Act and other statutes and executive orders that give the executive branch broad influence in the rulemaking of individual agencies. These are discussed in more detail in section G 1 a.

When an agency promulgates a final rule it must include a general statement of the basis and purpose of the rule. It must publish the rule for at least 30 days before the effective date except when (1) the rule (a) grants or recognizes an exemption or relieves a restriction or (b) is an interpretative rule or general statement of policy, or (2) the agency demonstrates good cause.

Beyond the text of the rule itself, perhaps the most important part of rulemaking is the statement of basis and purpose in the rule preamble. The preamble is the key document the public and the courts will use to construe the rule. A court will look first to the preamble to determine whether the agency has rationally explained the relationship between the underlying statute, the purpose of the rule, and the language of the rule itself. In the statement of basis and purpose, an agency must provide an adequate explanation of its reasons for adopting the rule. The Supreme Court has articulated this requirement as follows:

> The agency must examine the relevant data and articulate a satisfactory explanation of its action, including a "rational connection between the facts found and the choice made."[22]

In addition, most courts require the explanation to include a response to key comments received during the comment period. Some statutes, such as section 307(d)(6)(b) of the Clean Air Act, specifically require an agency to respond to significant comments. A reviewing court is held to a narrow standard of review of an agency's rulemaking decision. It may not substitute its judgment for that of the agency on the conclusions that can be drawn from the record, but it is to give the agency's decision a "hard look."[23] Courts will not, however, accept *post hoc* rationalizations to support an agency's position.[24]

2. Exceptions From APA Procedural Requirements

An agency may waive the requirements for public notice and comment for "good cause."[25] Although often considered a single test, the "good cause" exemption has three grounds for waiving public notice: that it is (1) impractical, (2) unnecessary, or (3) contrary to the public interest. Courts have not favored the "good cause" exception and thus construe it narrowly. As one commenter has noted, "[G]iven the importance Congress attached to the rulemaking process, it may be argued that decisions to omit it deserve the most careful scrutiny, especially in light of the delicate balancing courts are called upon to do."[26] Section 553(a) of the APA also does not require notice and comment when a proposed rule concerns a military or foreign affairs function of the United States, agency management or personnel, public property, loan, grant benefit, or contract.

E. DELEGATION AND DISCRETION

Unlike the legislative drafter, the administrative rule drafter is subject to statutory constraints. Congress or a state legislature must first delegate rulemaking authority to an agency, and the agency cannot act beyond the authority granted. The legislative body may also impose procedural and timing requirements. In addition, Congress has enacted certain generic requirements with which an agency must comply in exercising its rulemaking authority. These acts are discussed in section G 2.

Historically, courts have said that Congress is limited in the scope of authority it can or may delegate to another branch of government. Justice Harlan stated in 1892, "[T]hat Congress cannot delegate legislative power ... is a principle universally recognized as vital to the integrity and maintenance of the system of government ordained by the constitution."[27] Notwithstanding this general principle, the Supreme Court has consistently upheld an agency's authority to act even when Congress has provided only limited direction.[28]

Given the broad delegation of authority typically afforded an agency, the key question in judicial review of a rule is often whether the agency has correctly interpreted Congressional intent implementing a statute. During the 1970's and early 1980's, some courts freely substituted their judgment as to Congressional intent for that of the agency decisionmakers.[29] Courts freely substituted their judgment on legal interpretations made by agencies but granted deference on factual questions within the province of the agency's expertise. This type of deference is commonly referred to as "Skidmore deference" based on the doctrine enunciated by the Supreme Court in Skidmore v. Swift.[30] In a landmark decision in 1984, however, the Supreme Court rejected that approach and afforded agencies broad discretion in interpreting ambiguous statutory directives. In Chevron, U.S.A. Inc. v. NRDC,[31] the Supreme Court held that when Congress has not expressly stated a specific intent concerning the interpretative issue before the court, the role of the court on review is limited to determining whether the agency's interpretation of the statute is a reasonable one. The Court said, "[W]hen a challenge to an agency's construction of a statutory provision, fairly conceptualized, really centers on the wisdom of the agency's policy, rather than whether it is a reasonable choice within a gap left open by Congress, the challenge must fail."[32] The Court recognized that it was the role of the executive and not the judiciary to resolve policy choices that Congress intentionally or unintentionally did not resolve. Chevron has thus provided the administrative agency and its rule drafter substantial freedom to interpret an ambiguous provision of a statute.

F. RULEMAKING BY GUIDANCE AND POLICY

With all the additional requirements imposed by the APA, other specific statutory requirements, executive orders, and the increased litigation over rules adopted by agencies, executive branch agencies at the federal level have, in recent years, attempted to shape policy without the constraints of the rulemaking process. There has been a plethora of cases and scholarly commentary about when it is appropriate for agencies to issue guidances, interpretative rulings, and other nonlegislative rules to communicate with regulated entities and the public and when such action amounts to adopting a legislative rule without the benefit of the procedural requirements required by the APA or other relevant statutory directive. Courts have chastised agencies for failure to follow proper rulemaking procedures when their actions amount to legislative rules. The D.C. Circuit, in a rebuke of EPA's efforts to issue a "guidance" under the Clean Air Act, aptly summarized the view that agencies have gone too far in circumventing the APA:

> The phenomenon we see in this case is familiar. Congress passes a broadly worded statute. The agency follows with regulations containing broad language, open-ended phrases, ambiguous standards and the like. Then as years pass, the agency issues circulars or guidance or memoranda, explaining, interpreting, defining and often expanding the commands in the regulations. One guidance document may yield another and then another and so on. Several words in a regulation may spawn hundreds of pages of text as the agency offers more and more detail regarding what its regulations demand of regulated entities. Law is made, without notice and comment, without public participants, and without publication in the Federal Register or the Code of Federal Regulations.[33]

Courts, however, faced with potential challenges to every agency pronouncement are constantly trying to balance the agency's ability to do its job and implement the statutory and regulatory scheme without having to undertake a rulemaking for every interpretation, applicability determination, or other agency statement.[34]

G. EXECUTIVE AND LEGISLATIVE CHECKS ON RULEMAKING

Significant differences exist between federal and state executive and legislative checks on rulemaking. For this reason, each is addressed separately in this section.

1. Executive

a. Federal

The federal APA does not contain a provision for executive branch oversight of the rulemaking process. Notwithstanding, one of the most controversial aspects of administrative law development in recent years has been the increased role of the White House in the rulemaking process.[35] The principal basis for White House review is Executive Order 12,291, issued by President Reagan in the early days of his administration. The purpose of the order is "to reduce the burdens of existing and future regulations, increase agency accountability for regulatory actions, minimize duplication and conflict of regulations, and insure well-reasoned regulations."[36]

The executive order covers all major rules.[37] The order requires the agency to perform a regulatory impact analysis (RIA) of the rule. The analysis sets out the costs and benefits of the rule. In addition, the analysis must describe alternative approaches that could achieve substantially the same goal and explain why the alternatives were not adopted.

For a major rule the agency must submit the RIA to the Office of Management and Budget (OMB) at least sixty days prior to publication of the proposed rule. For minor rules, the agency must afford OMB a ten-day review period. Although these timetables do not seem extraordinary, extensive delay often results because OMB suspends review of the rule. Furthermore, even if the time period has run, agencies are often reluctant to issue rules without OMB clearance. An agency may proceed, however, if regulatory review will delay promulgation of a rule beyond a statutory or court-ordered deadline.[38]

In addition to Executive Order 12,291, several other executive orders—numbers 12,630, 12,612, and 12,498—require review of agency rules. Executive Order 13,132 issued by President Clinton in 1995 addresses federalism issues.[39] It requires that an agency not promulgate any regulation that has federalism implications and preempts state law, unless the agency has consulted with state officials, and in a separately identified section of the preamble, provides to the Director of the Office of Management and Budget a summary impact statement on federalism issues. This impact statement must include why the regulation needs to be adopted and how any concerns raised by state officials were addressed. Executive Order 13045 issued in 1997 directs most federal agencies when developing regulations to conduct an evaluation of the environmental, health, or safety effects of the planned regulation on children and provide an explanation of how the planned regulation is preferable to other feasible alternatives.[40]

In addition to enabling legislation and executive orders, the federal administrative rule drafter should also be aware of several other statutory constraints on administrative rulemaking. For example, Congress enacted the Paperwork Reduction Act (PWRA)[41] as part of an effort at regulatory reform to ease paperwork requirements on regulated parties. The Act applies to a rule that imposes information collection requirements. The Act does not prohibit an agency from adopting a particular type of rule. It does, however, require the agency to obtain clearance of OMB and justify the use of information collection.[42] It also requires an agency to estimate the amount of person hours and paperwork the rule will require. The agency must provide support to justify its information demands and convince OMB that it has done everything possible to minimize the reporting burden. By using this screening mechanism, Congress has given OMB direct oversight in the rulemaking process.[43] In addition, the Act requires the agency to notify the public that it may file comments on the information collection requirements with OMB.

The Regulatory Flexibility Act[44] also limits the administrative rule drafter by requiring an agency to analyze the impact of the rule on small entities, including small businesses and municipalities. The Act applies to all rules subject to the informal rulemaking requirements of section 553 of the APA. Like the PWRA, it does not mandate or prohibit a particular type of rule. Rather, it requires the agency to consider alternatives that may have less impact on small entities and explain why those alternatives were rejected. The agency may also certify that the rule does not have a significant adverse impact on small entities and avoid a regulatory flexibility analysis. If a rule would have an impact on small entities, the agency must publish an initial analysis with the proposed rule. The Act also requires special notification procedures to afford small entities the opportunity to participate in the comment process. Once the comment period closes, a final analysis must address the comments received.

The Unfunded Mandates Reform Act of 1995[45] (UMRA) establishes requirements for federal agencies to assess the efforts of their regulatory actions on state, local, and tribal governments. The UMRA was enacted as part of the "Gingrich revolution" reform effort in response to concerns from state governments that the federal government was imposing requirements on them without providing funding for the same. Agencies have to develop a cost-benefit analysis for rules with "federal mandates" that may result in expenditures to state, local, or tribal governments in the aggregate, or to the private sector, of $100 million in any one year.

As a practical matter, the regulatory flexibility analysis often becomes intertwined with the analysis required under Executive Order 12,291, discussed earlier in this subsection.

b. State

As is the case with the federal APA the 1961 version of the Model State Administrative Procedure Act (MSAPA) did not provide for executive branch oversight of the rulemaking process. Many states have nevertheless enacted these provisions and as a result they are included in the 1981 MSAPA.[46]

Section 3–202(a) of the MSAPA authorizes the governor to suspend or rescind an agency rule (or severable portion of a rule) to the same extent that the agency itself can. Unlike many legislative veto provisions, the MSAPA does not place a time limit on the exercise of the governor's authority. In exercising the authority the governor must follow the same procedural requirements as an agency in adopting a rule and thus must provide an explanation of the action and submit to a public comment process.

The MSAPA also authorizes the governor to terminate a pending rulemaking proceeding. The governor must, however, provide an explanation for the action. In addition, the MSAPA provides for an administrative rules counsel. The counsel serves as the liaison with the state agencies and seeks to resolve differences between an agency and the executive before a rule is issued in an effort to make the state rulemaking process less cumbersome and duplicative. Without this type of effort an agency could go through the entire rulemaking process only to have the governor rescind the rule.

The role of the executive in rulemaking at the state level is far more established than at the federal level, although presidential involvement in the rulemaking process is certainly alive and well. The state rule drafter must be aware of the role of the governor's office in the drafter's state. Most states have some type of formalized executive review process recognized by statute.

2. Legislative

a. Federal

Unlike typical states discussed in the next subsection, Congressional oversight of rules is minimal. Although for many years a common provision in federal statutes granting rulemaking authority permitted either house of Congress to veto a rule adopted by an agency, these provisions were struck down by the Supreme Court in Immigration and Naturalization Service v. Chadha.[47] In Chadha the court found unconstitutional a statute authorizing one house of Congress to overturn an administrative action undertaken by the Attorney General. The Court indicated that a legislative veto of an agency action was unconstitutional unless Congress did so by means that satisfied Constitutional requirements for a law, including passage by both houses and the availability of presidential veto. When it follows that route, Congress is exercising its ultimate authority over rules by in effect amending the statute authorizing the rulemaking.

However, as part of Congress' increasing scrutiny over the broad exercise of powers by executive branch agencies, Congress in 1996 passed legislation requiring an agency to submit a report to each house of Congress on a rule along with a cost benefit analysis and regulatory impacts analysis, the agency's actions related to the UMRA, and other relevant information.[48] Following submission of the report, the statute provides, with limited exceptions, that if Congress passes a joint resolution of disapproval within a specified time period, the rule shall have no force and effect.[49] These provisions were added by Congress as part of the reform efforts following the 1994 Congressional elections and the "Gingrich revolution" to restrain the federal executive branch.

b. State

Unlike the federal APA, sections 3–203 and 3–204 of the MSAPA contain an express mechanism for legislative review of state rulemaking that is less than full legislative enactment by both state houses subject to veto. Many states have also enacted various legislative review provisions.[50] The typical mechanism, and the one included in the MSAPA, is a single standing committee consisting of members of both houses of the state legislature. If the committee objects to a rule because it believes it to be beyond the procedural or substantive authority of the adopting agency, the committee files an objection with the secretary of state. The state agency then has fourteen days to respond in writing to the committee, whereupon the committee may modify or withdraw its objection. If the objection is not withdrawn, the burden is upon the agency in a proceeding for judicial review or enforcement of the rule to establish that the whole or the portion of the rule objected to is within the procedural and substantive authority delegated to the agency. The advantages and disadvantages of this legislative role in the state administrative process are explored by Arthur Bonfield in his treatise on state administrative law.[51]

H. CONCLUSION

The informal rulemaking process is anything but an easy way to develop an administrative rule. Public participation and involvement by other governmental entities makes the process time consuming and cumbersome. The rule drafter has many constraints on developing a rule. Nevertheless, the process is designed to lead to a workable rule. On occasion it does, but the realities of the process of public participation and the agency's desire for the rule to withstand judicial scrutiny often lead to complex and technical rules that are difficult to understand and follow. Frequently, the rule drafter will doubt whether the rule finally adopted passes the basic goal enunciated in the introduction to this chapter: to set forth precisely (1) who may or may not do something and (2) what that person may or may not do.

Endnotes

1. 5 U.S.C.A. § 551 et seq.

2. Some commentators have criticized this development. Tabler & Shere, EPA's Practice of Regulation–By–Memo, 5 Nat. Res. & Env., No.2, 5 (1990) states: "Regulation-by-memo lacks any of this public character. In short, where Congress fails to provide specific policy guidance, the regulatory notice and comment process is an uneasy part of our democratic system. The regulation-by-memo 'process' should not be a part of the system at all."

3. Consistent with the general theme of this, in 1998, then President Clinton issued an Executive Directive to federal agencies and departments to "make the Government more responsive, accessible, and understandable with it's communications with the public." The Memorandum directed agency drafters to "use plain language in all proposed and final rulemaking documents published in the Federal Register," and to use common every day words, voice, pronouns and short sentences. William J. Clinton, "Memorandum For The Heads of Executive Departments and Agencies," June 1, 1998; copy of Memorandum available at www:plainlanguage.gov/cites/memo.htm.

4. 5 U.S.C.A. § 551(4).

5. 5 U.S.C.A. § 553(b).

6. The Attorney General's Manual on the APA 30, n.3 (1947) (1971 Reprint).

7. McLouth Steel Products Corp. v. Thomas, 838 F.2d 1317 (D.C. Cir. 1988) (quoting Community Nutrition v. Young, 818 F.2d 943 (D.C. Cir. 1987)).

8. 1 K. Davis, Administrative Law 450 (2d ed. 1978).

9. For a thorough discussion of state requirements, see Bonfield, State Administrative Rule Making (1986).

10. Harter, Negotiating Regulations: A Cure for Malaise, 71 Geo. L. J. 1 (1982).

11. P.L. 101–648. The new provisions are to be codified at 5 U.S.C.A. §§ 581–590. The Environmental Protection Agency has already announced it is considering development of a rule in accordance with the act. See 56 Fed. Reg. 5167 (Feb. 8, 1991).

12. For a discussion of some of these efforts, see Burns, The Evolving Role of Dispute Resolution in Administrative Procedures, 5 Nat. Res. & Env. No.2, 26, 28 (1990). See also Pritzker, Working Together for Better Regulations, 5 Nat. Res. & Env. No.2, 29 (1990). The Administrative Conference of the United States has recommended procedures for establishing an appropriate regulatory negotiation process. See 1 C.F.R. 305.85-5. See also 56 Fed. Reg. 5167 (Feb. 8, 1991).

13. See, e.g., Toxic Substances Control Act, 15 U.S.C.A. § 2670.

14. E.g., Occupational Safety and Health Act, 29 U.S.C.A. § 655(b)(3); Clean Air Act, 42 U.S.C.A. § 7607(d).

15. 42 U.S.C.A. § 7607(d).

16. 15 U.S.C.A. § 2058(f)(3).

17. 42 U.S.C.A. § 7607(d).

18. E.g., 29 U.S.C.A. § 655(f); 15 U.S.C.A. 57a(e)(3).

19. For a discussion of the line of cases in which courts, most notably the D.C. circuit, imposed additional procedural requirements on agencies, see Davis, supra, note 9 at § 6.12.

20. 435 U.S. 519, 98 S.Ct. 1197 (1978).

21. Courts have enunciated the "logical outgrowth" in various ways at various times and there is uncertainty as to how much of the change can be a logical outgrowth of a comment received as compared to the logical outgrowth of the proposal itself. Compare Small Refiner Lead Phase–Down Task Force v. EPA, 705 F.2d 506, 549 (D.C. Cir. 1983) (notice can not be bootstrapped from a comment; agency itself must put public on notice) with City of Stoughton v. EPA, 858 F. 2d 747, 753 (D.C. Cir. 1988) (test is whether changes are a logical outgrowth of proposal notice and comments).

22. Motor Vehicle Manufacturers Ass'n. v. State Farm Mutual Automobile Ins. Co., 463 U.S. 29, 43, 103 S.Ct. 2856, 2866 (1983) (quoting Burlington Truck Lines Inc. v. U.S., 371 U.S. 156, 168, 83 S.Ct. 239, 245–46 (1962)).

23. Small Refiner Lead Phase-Down Task Force v. E.P.A., 705 F.2d 506, 520 (D.C. Cir. 1983).

24. Motor Vehicle Manufacturers Ass'n v. State Farm Mutual Automobile Ins. Co., 463 U.S. at 50, 103 S.Ct. at 2870.

25. Mobay Chemical Corp. v. Gorsuch, 682 F.2d 419, 426 (3rd Cir. 1982). For a comprehensive review of the good cause exception see Jordan, The ABA's Good Cause Exemption, 36 Administrative L. Rev. 113 (1984).

26. Jordan, supra note 26, at 120.

27. Field v. Clark, 143 U.S. 649, 692, 12 S.Ct. 495, 504 (1892).

28. See discussion of cases in Modjeska, Administrative Law & Practice § 1.4–1.6 (1982).

29. Motor Vehicle Manufacturers Ass'n v. State Farm Mutual Automobile Insurance Co., 463 U.S. 29, 103 S. Ct. 2856 (1983). For a general discussion of the case law see Davis, supra note 9, at § 29.16.

30. 323 U.S. 134 (1944).

31. 467 U.S. 837, 104 S.Ct. 2778 (1984).

32. Id. at 865–66, 104 S.Ct. at 2793.

33. Appalachian Power Co. v. EPA, 208 F.3d 1015, 1020 (D.D. Cir. 2000).

34. There are a number of interesting articles on finding this balance when agency action is a valid nonlegislative pronouncement and when an agency should be required to adhere to notice and comment rulemaking procedures. *See e.g.* P. Strauss, *Publication Rules in the Rulemaking Spectrum: Assuring Proper Respect for an Essential Element*, 53 Admin. L. Rev. 803 (2001); W. Funk, *When is a "Rule" a Regulation? Making a Clear Line*

Between Nonlegislative Rules and Legislative Rules, 54 Admin. L. Rev. 659 (2002); R. Anthony, *Interpretative Rules, Policy Statements, Guidances, Manuals, and the Like—Should Federal Agencies Use Them to Bind the Public?*, 41 Duke L. Journal 1311 (1992).

35. See, Strauss & Sunstein, The Role of the President and OMB in Informal Rulemaking, 38 Admin. L. Rev. 181 (1986); Bruff, Presidential Management of Agency Rulemaking, 57 Geo. Wash. L. Rev. 533 (1989); Rosenberg, Beyond The Limits of Executive Power: Presidential Control of Agency Rulemaking Under Executive Order 12,291, Vol. 80 Mich. L. Rev. 193 (1981).

36. 46 Fed. Reg. 13,193 (1981).

37. A "major" rule is defined as one which will have an annual effect on the economy of greater than $1 million, a major increase in costs or prices, or significant adverse effects on competition, employment, or other aspects of the economy. Executive Order 12,291 § 1(b).

38. Environmental Defense Fund v. Thomas, 627 F. Supp. 566 (D.D.C. 1986).

39. Exec. Order 13,132, "Federalism," 64 Fed. Reg. 43,255 (Aug. 4, 1999).

40. Exec. Order 13,045, "Protection of Children From Environmental Health Rules and Safety Rules," 62 Fed. Reg. 19,885 (Apr. 23, 1997).

41. 44 U.S.C.A. §§ 3501–20.

42. See O'Reilly, Administrative Rulemaking § 10.02 (1983).

43. The Paperwork Reduction Act implementation rules are set forth at 53 Fed. Reg. 16,618 (1988).

44. 5 U.S.C.A. § 601 et seq.

45. 2 U.S.C. § 1501 (1995); Pub. L. 104–4.

46. For a more complete discussion of the model act and state rulemaking, see Bonfield, supra note 10.

47. 462 U.S. 919, 103 S.Ct. 2764 (1983).

48. 5 U.S.C. § 801(a). Added as Pub. L. 104–121, title II, Sec. 251 (Mar. 29, 1996), 110 Stat. 868.

49. Id.

50. See Bonfield, supra note 10, at § 8.3.1 n.5 for a survey of state provisions.

51. See Bonfield, supra note 10, at § 8.1.2.

Chapter 16

COURT RULES

A. SUBJECT AREAS

Courts make rules governing four principal areas—procedure, court administration, the legal profession, and judges.

Procedure may be defined as the means by which a right created by substantive law is asserted in the courts.[1] Procedural rules are usually divided by type of proceeding—e.g., civil, criminal, evidence, appellate, supreme court, probate, juvenile, domestic relations, and traffic. Each jurisdiction does not have every type of rule, but almost every state has at least civil, criminal, and appellate rules. The primary function of these rules is to govern what litigants and their lawyers do in the filing of pleadings and other papers in court and in the conduct of court proceedings.

A continuing problem in procedural rulemaking is the distinction between procedure and substantive rights. Traditional separation of powers doctrine holds that the former is within the courts' rulemaking power but the latter are excluded from it. Unfortunately, there is not always a bright line to distinguish one from the other.[2] The United States Supreme Court, after wrestling with the problem in several cases, finally developed the practical test that if a matter is arguably procedural and is the subject of a rule adopted by the Court upon recommendation of its advisory committee on rules and without objection by Congress, the rule is valid.[3] This is so even if the matter is also arguably substantive.

In addition to the possible overlap between substance and procedure, a similar overlap can also exist between procedure and administration. Court administration is generally defined as relating to matters of internal concern of the courts.[4] What a court does internally can have a substantial effect on litigants, and actions of litigants likewise affect a court's internal operations. The American Bar Association's Court Organization Standards in section 1.32 define court administration to include court calendars, assignment of judges, duties of court staff, internal administration, and financial administration. Additional matters may include general superintendence of lower courts, and court facilities and security.

The legal profession for regulation purposes includes everything that relates to the practice of law including admission, discipline, ethics, and competence. Regulation of the legal profession affects and is affected by both procedural and administrative rules but is usually easy to separate from both. Rules governing admission to the bar cover educational and character requirements and the bar examination. Standards of conduct of attorneys are established in rules or canons of professional conduct, while the enforcement machinery is often established in separate rules. In recent years court rules have also covered topics such as mandatory membership in a state bar association, mandatory continuing legal education, and a client security fund.[5]

The fourth area subject to court rules is the judges themselves. Most jurisdictions today have rules that establish a code of judicial conduct, enforcement of judicial discipline, and some even have mandatory judicial education.[6]

For each of the last three areas—court administration, legal profession, and judges—the legislature or courts have set up administrative structures. Court administration rules are administered by administrative judges and by state and local court administrators. The legal profession rules usually require at least two separate agencies, one covering admission and the other discipline, although the two can be combined in a single agency. Judicial conduct and discipline also requires at least one separate agency and sometimes two.[7] Mandatory continuing education for lawyers may be administered by the discipline agency or a separate body. For judges, the mandatory education program is usually administered by the state court administrator's office.

B. AUTHORITY

Courts can point to three separate sources for their rulemaking authority—constitutional, inherent, and statutory. There has long been a debate over whether procedural rulemaking is properly a part of the judicial power, the legislative power, or both.[8] Part of the disagreement may result from the fact that procedural rules can be of two types. One type is applicable nationwide in the case of federal courts and statewide for state courts. The second is local, applicable only in a particular court. A supreme court adopts the former to govern proceedings in all inferior courts, while the latter is adopted by a court to govern its own proceedings. A court is almost always held to have the inherent power to regulate its own proceedings, subject to general rules adopted by a supreme court or legislature. The basic dispute is over the relative authority of the supreme court and the legislature to adopt statewide rules.

In the federal system the U.S. Supreme Court has never asserted constitutional or inherent authority to adopt procedural rules for the federal appellate and trial courts. When it does so, the court always cites the 1934 Rules Enabling Act for its authority. In some states, by contrast, the supreme court has claimed inherent authority to adopt general procedural rules. In a substantial number of states, the constitution have expressly granted general procedural rulemaking authority to the supreme court. In others the legislature has expressly delegated the authority by statute. Often the constitution or a statute will mandate that the supreme court submit proposed rules to the legislature to give it an opportunity to reject or amend them. In some states a court adopted procedural rule can repeal an inconsistent statute. In almost every state an accommodation has been worked out that gives primary responsibility for control of procedure to the supreme court but preserves some opportunity for the legislature to modify a rule.[9]

Another area of conflict between the courts and legislatures has been over control of the legal profession. During most of the nineteenth century, legislatures were the primary actors in regulation of the legal profession, just as they were for procedure. At the end of that century, however, courts began to assert an inherent power to regulate the legal profession, either superior to or to the exclusion of the legislature. This movement has grown stronger in the twentieth century. Over the past several decades, a number of states amended their constitutions to give expressly to their supreme courts either the exclusive or paramount power to regulate the legal profession. If the power is exclusive, a statute attempting to regulate the legal profession is held to be unconstitutional. If the supreme court interprets its power to be only paramount, then a statute on the subject is held to be unconstitutional only if the court finds that the legislation interferes with the supreme court's power over the subject area. One test commonly applied is that a supreme court will accept a statute that imposes a higher standard than the supreme court rule, but not a standard that is lower. The movement to court regulation has been so strong that by the end of the 1980's the superior power of a supreme court to regulate the legal profession was recognized in all but one or two states.[10] In the federal courts, the matter is still unresolved.[11]

The administrative role of supreme courts or boards of judges has developed only in the past half century, and particularly in the past two decades. Prior to the 1930's, there was no effort to administer courts on a national or state wide basis. Each court acted independently and in the states was funded separately, with no effort at control by the supreme court. In the 1930's, however, persons concerned with the courts began to recognize that some type of centralized administration was desirable. The first step was to create an administrative office of the courts with a director. Often the initial role was primarily statistical, but as time went on it expanded into budget development, personnel, supplies, and judicial assignments. The entire effort was usually done with legislative authorization. After World War II, a movement developed to give express constitutional authority over administration of the judicial branch to state supreme courts and state chief justices. As a result, supreme courts began to adopt administrative rules for entire state systems.[12] A related development has been to fund courts entirely by the state rather than all or partially by local units of government. In the administrative area, there have been only a few conflicts between the courts and the legislatures, with the courts almost always winning. Even in the area of finances, courts have asserted power to compel funding of the courts to the extent the courts think is essential to their functioning as courts.[13] Judicial salaries are one area over which legislatures are conceded to be paramount.

C. PROCESS

Interest in the process by which supreme courts adopt rules has been directly related to the extent to which courts exercise rulemaking power. Initially, when a court adopted rules only for its own procedures, the court merely issued the rules without any type of consultation, pre adoption publication, or hearing. Courts treated the rulemaking process as something entirely internal. As supreme courts expanded their rulemaking activities, however, public interest in those activities grew. Some but not all supreme courts responded by appointing advisory committees, publishing proposed rules and soliciting comments on them, and even holding hearings on the proposals. Some states established by statute advisory groups on rules, specifying the manner in which members were selected and the interests they were to represent. These groups were often called judicial councils.[14] The 1970's, which saw a substantial increase in rulemaking by supreme courts, also saw a substantial criticism of their rulemaking procedures because they were not open and accessible to the public or interested parties.[15] As a result of this criticism, the process in the federal system and in many states was made more open with greater opportunity for public participation. The most common steps were the appointment of an advisory committee and publication of proposed rules with a request for comments. It should be noted that supreme courts usually appoint advisory committees only for procedural rules. The supreme courts may use their commissions on admission or discipline of lawyers or judges to advise them on rules covering those areas. These groups often propose rules to the supreme courts on their own initiative. There are seldom standing advisory committees on administrative rules, but ad hoc committees may be appointed.

One area in which the courts have not improved is in the use of professionally trained or experienced drafters to prepare their rules. The situation described in section A as to the U.S. Supreme Court's advisory committee on rules is representative of or even better than in most states. The federal committee, at least, uses reporters who are experts in the substantive areas of the rules, even if not expert drafters. It has also appointed a committee on style to review proposed rules from a good drafting perspective. At the state level, the rules committees may not divide themselves into subcommittees for each type of rule such as civil or criminal, the committees or subcommittees may not have reporters, and if they do, they may not be experts in the substantive areas for which they are responsible. They are very unlikely to have any expertise in drafting. A supreme court itself is also not likely to have a person on its staff who is an expert drafter. The result is that most court rules suffer from all of the weaknesses ascribed to legal writing in general.

In the federal system and in many states, intermediate appellate courts and trial courts are expressly or by tradition authorized to issue local procedural rules. Many federal district courts also have rules governing admission to practice in those courts, there being no national admitting authority for federal courts. Federal courts of appeals have only recently appointed rules advisory committees, but the extent to which they either publish proposed rules and solicit comments in them is still uneven. The district courts seldom have advisory committees and even less seldom seek comments on proposed rules. The U.S. Supreme Court and state supreme courts act similarly as to practice in their own courts.

Endnotes

1. F. James & G. Hazard, Civil Procedure § 1.1 (3d ed. 1985).

2. Guaranty Trust Co. v. York, 326 U.S. 99, 108, 65 S.Ct. 1464, 1469 (1945).

3. Hanna v. Plumer, 380 U.S. 460, 85 S. Ct. 1136 (1965).

4. American Bar Association, Standards Relating to Court Organization sec. 1.31 (1990).

5. For an effort to distinguish between procedure, court administration, and the legal profession, see C. Grau, Judicial Rulemaking: Administration, Access and Accountability 3–4 (1978).

6. J. Shaman, S. Lubet, and J. Alfini, Judicial Conduct and Ethics (1990).

7. I. Tesitor and D. Sinks, Judicial Conduct Organizations (2d ed. 1980); K. Carr and L. Bergson, Literature on Judicial Conduct (1979).

8. See F. Stumpf, Inherent Powers of the Courts: Sword and Shield of the Judiciary, National Judiciary College (1994); Wolf, Inherent Rulemaking Authority of an Independent Judiciary, 56 U. Miami L. Rev. 507 (2002): Levin and Amsterdam, Legislative Control Over Judicial Rulemaking: A Problem in Constitutional Revision, 107 Pennsylvania L. Rev. 1 (1958).

9. C. Grau, supra note 5, at 7–22.

10. R. Martineau, Regulation of the Legal Profession: The Relationship Between Judicial and Legislative Power (1987) (published as a report of the National Center for State Courts).

11. See Zacharias and Green, Federal Court Authority to Regulate Lawyers: A Practice in Search of a Theory, 56 Vanderbilt Law Review 1303 (2003) commenting on the implications of United States v. Williams, 504 U.S. 36 (1992).

12. A. Vanderbilt, Minimum Standards of Judicial Administration (1949); American Bar Association, Standards Relating to Court Organization (1974); C. Grau, supra note 5, at 23–48.

13. See Note, The Courts' Inherent Power to Compel Legislative Funding of Judicial Functions, 81 Mich. L. Rev. 1687 (1983). A recent example was in New York. See Glaser, Wachtler v. Cuomo: The Limits of Inherent Powers, 78 Judicature 12 (1994).

14. McKay, Use of Judicial Councils and Conferences, in American Bar Association, The Improvement of the Administration of Justice 113–126 (6th ed. 1981).

15. J. Weinstein, Reform of Court Rule–Making Procedures (1977); G. Grau, supra note 48, at 49–66.

Appendix

DRAFTING EXAMPLES

The following drafting examples are drawn from existing statutes and rules without attributing the source. The statute or rule first appears in plain type as incorrectly drafted and is followed by a revision in *italics* that applies the applicable rule.

CHAPTER 6: THE WHO—THE ACTOR

A. Use the Singular

[original]

Retail establishments may not sell tobacco products to minors under age 16.

[revised]

A retail establishment may not sell a tobacco product to a person under age 16.

B. Identify the Actor

Executions of the death penalty shall take place on the day designated by the judge passing sentence.

The director shall carry out a death sentence on the day designated in the sentence.

C. Use Articles as Modifiers

1. Use "*A*" or "*An*" Rather than "*Any*," "*Each*," "*Every*," or "*No*"

If any individual is ineligible for extended benefits . . .

If an individual is ineligible for extended benefits . . .

2. Use "*The*" Rather than "*Such*" or "*Said*"

Said husband and wife cannot, by any such contract with each other, alter their legal relations, except that they may agree to such immediate separation and make such provisions for the support of either of them and their children during such separation.

The husband and wife may not alter their legal relations by a contract with each other, except for agreeing to an immediate separation and to support provisions for themselves and their children during the separation.

D. Limit the Use of Pronouns

The President may delegate the authority granted to him in the preceding section to the Secretary of State.

The president may delegate the authority granted in the preceding section to the secretary of state.

E. List or Characterize Multiple Actors

Electric generating plants, petroleum refineries, gasification plants, facilities used for the transportation conversion, treatment, transfer, or storage of liquified natural gas, oil and gas facilities, and pipelines and transmission facilities shall comply with the standards listed in Chapter 33 of Title 16.

In the definition section:

"Energy facility" means an electric generating plant, petroleum refinery, gasification plant, or property or equipment used for the transportation conversion, treatment, transfer, transmission, or storage of oil, gas, natural gas, or electricity.

In the body of the statute:

An energy facility shall comply with chapter 33, title 16.

F. Save the Negative for the Action

No person shall receive, retain, or dispose of property of another, knowing or having reasonable cause to believe that the property has been obtained through commission of a theft offense.

A person may not receive, retain, or dispose of property of another, knowing or having reasonable cause to believe the property was stolen.

CHAPTER 7: THE WHAT—THE ACTION
AND OBJECT OR COMPLEMENT

A. The Action

1. Use Active Voice

A decision on the matter will be rendered by the agency within 30 days

The agency shall decide the matter within 30 days.

2. Use Base Verbs

Every owner's policy of liability insurance shall designate by explicit description or by appropriate reference all motor vehicles with respect to which coverage is thereby granted.

An owner's policy of liability insurance must describe or refer explicitly to a motor vehicle covered by the policy.

3. Use the Present Tense and the Indicative Mood

If a married woman were to be the subject of a nonspousal artificial insemination and if her husband consented to the artificial insemination, the husband shall be treated in law and regarded as the natural father of a child conceived as a result of the artificial insemination.

If a married woman undergoes a nonspousal artificial insemination with her husband's consent, for legal purposes the husband has the status of the natural father of the child conceived by the artificial insemination.

4. Use "*Shall*" Only to Impose a Duty to Act

A motion for reconsideration shall be filed not later than ten days after the date of the order.

A party seeking reconsideration shall file a motion within 10 days of the order's date.

5. Use "*May*" to Grant Discretion or Authority to Act.

If a state furnishes support to an individual to whom a duty of support is owed, it shall have the right to initiate a proceeding for the purpose of securing reimbursement for support.

If a state furnishes support to a person, it may seek reimbursement of the support furnished.

6. Use "*May Not*" to Prohibit an Action

No person shall cause or knowingly permit any minor under eighteen to drive a motor vehicle upon a highway as an operator, unless such minor has first obtained a license or permit to drive a motor vehicle.

A person may not permit a minor to drive a motor vehicle on a highway unless the minor first obtains a driver's license or permit.

7. Use the Positive Rather than the Negative

Before the expiration of this period, the physician may not destroy such confidential information and written consent form.

Before the expiration of this period, the physician shall retain the confidential information and written consent form.

8. Tabulation for Multiple Actions

[See example of tabulation in chapter 8, section G]

B. The Object of the Verb or the Complement of the Actor

Beginning on the first day of the pay period within which the employee completes the prescribed probationary period in his classification with the state, each employee shall receive automatic salary adjustments equivalent to the next higher step within the pay range for his class or grade.

From the first day of the pay period after the employee completes the probationary period in the employee's state classification, the director of administrative services shall pay an automatic salary adjustment to the employee equivalent to the next higher step within the pay range for the employee's class or grade.

CHAPTER 8: GENERAL RULES

A. Use Only Necessary Words

1. Introduction

[No example]

2. Identify Working Words and Glue Words

The department shall review the completed forms, and shall determine whether the information included by the biological parent is of a type permissible under division (D)(2) and (3) of section 3107.12 of the Revised Code and, to the best of its ability, whether the information is accurate.

The department shall determine whether a completed form includes accurate and permissible types of information under Revised Code sections (2) 3107.12(D) (2) and (3).

3. Avoid Compound Constructions or Expressions

The magistrate must give consideration to the issue as to whether to allow the extension.

The magistrate shall consider whether to allow the extension.

4. Avoid Redundant Legal Phrases

The parties must give a full and complete description of their intended actions.

A party shall give a complete description of the intended action.

B. Use Common Words

[No example]

C. Avoid Lawyerisms

Prior to the issuance of said initial license and annually thereafter, the party who grants the license therefore shall inspect each public swimming pool, public spa, or special use pool in his jurisdiction to thereby determine whether or not such pool or spa is in compliance with the code.

Before issuance of the initial license and annually while the license is in effect, the licensor shall inspect each public swimming pool, public spa, or special use pool in the jurisdiction to determine if the pool or spa is in compliance with the code.

D. Be Consistent

As used in this Chapter, "employee," "workman," or "operator" means a person in the service of the state or a county.

As used in this chapter, "employee" means a person in the service of the state or a county, including a worker or operator.

E. Use Short Sentences

An officer of an agency of the state or of a political subdivision acting in his representative capacity, or any person who is or will be aggrieved or adversely affected by a violation which has occurred, is occurring, or will occur may file a complaint, in writing and verified by the affidavit of the complainant, his agent, or attorney, with the director of environmental protection, in accordance with the rules of the director adopted pursuant to Chapter 119 of the Revised Code, alleging that another person has violated, is violating, or will violate any law, rule, standard, or order relating to air pollution, water pollution, solid waste, public water supply, or hazardous waste, or, if the person is in possession of a valid license, permit, variance, or plan approval relating to air pollution, water pollution, solid waste, public water supply, or hazardous waste, that the person has violated, is violating, or will violate the conditions of such license, permit, variance or plan approval.

A person may file a complaint with the director of environmental protection in accordance with the rules of the director adopted under chapter 119 of the Revised Code. The person shall file the complaint in writing, verified by an affidavit of the complainant, its agent, or attorney. The complaint must allege a past, present, or future violation of a law, rule, standard, order, condition of a license, permit, variance, or plan approval, relating to air or water pollution, solid waste, public water supply, or hazardous waste.

F. Arrange Words Carefully

A court, when it appears that his health or safety may be in danger, may take a child into custody.

If a child's health or safety may be in danger, a court may take the child into custody.

G. Tabulate to Simplify

The applicant for a permit issued under this section shall include the date and starting time of the match or exhibition, the address of the place where the match or exhibition is to be held, the name of the contestants and their seconds, the seating capacity of the building or hall where the exhibition is to be held, the admission charge or any other charges, the amount of compensation or percentage of gate receipts to be paid to each contestant, the name and address of the applicant, and the serial number of the applicant's promoter's license.

The applicant for a permit issued under this section shall include the:

(a) date and starting time of the match or exhibition;

(b) address and seating capacity of the building or hall where the match or exhibition is to be held;

(c)   name of the contestants and their seconds;

(d)   admission charge or any other charges;

(e)   amount of compensation or percentage of gate receipts to be paid to each contestant;

(f)   name and address of the applicant; and

(g)   serial number of the applicant's promoter's license.

"California style"

The applicant for a permit issued under this section shall include all of the following information:

(a)   The date and starting time of the match or exhibition.

(b)   The address and seating capacity of the building or hall where the match or exhibition is to be held.

(c)   The name of the contestants and their seconds.

(d)   The admission charge or any other charges.

(e)   The amount of compensation or percentage of gate receipts to be paid to each contestant.

(f)   The name and address of the applicant.

(g)   The serial number of the applicant's promoter's license.

H.   Punctuate Properly

The ancillary receiver shall arrange a date for a hearing if necessary under section 3903.39 of the Revised Code, and shall give notice to the liquidator in the domiciliary state, either by certified mail, or by personal service at least forty days prior to the date set for hearing.

The ancillary receiver shall arrange a date for a hearing if necessary under Revised Code section 3903.39 and shall give notice to the liquidator in the domiciliary state, either by certified mail or by personal service, at least forty days prior to the hearing.

I.   Definitions

A "medical prescription" is a prescription received from a medical doctor.

"Prescription" means a medical doctor's written order for the preparation and use of a medicine or remedy.

J.   Conditions, Exceptions, and Provisos

1.   Conditions

The board of health of the city or general health district shall provide, for all persons confined in such a house or place, food, fuel, and all other necessaries of life, including medical attendance, medicine, and nurses when necessary, when a house or other place is quarantined because of contagious diseases.

If a house or other place is quarantined because of a contagious disease, the board of health of the city or general health district shall provide necessaries of life, including food, fuel, medical attendance, medicine, and nursing care, for a person confined in the quarantined house or place.

2. Exceptions

A person owning a cat or dog shall have the animal neutered within six months of the later of (a) the date of this statute, (b) the animal's birth, or (c) the date the owner acquires the animal unless the person is granted a breeding permit under subsection d.

Except for an owner granted a breeding permit under subsection d, the owner of a cat or dog shall have the animal neutered within six months of the later of:

(a)   the date of this statute,

(b)   the animal's birth, or

(c)   the date the owner acquires the animal.

3. Provisos

After a lapse of one year from the date of such designation, such declarant may have such designation vacated or changed by filing in said probate court an application to vacate or change such designation of heir; provided, that there is compliance with the procedure, conditions, and prerequisites required in the making of the original declaration.

If a declarant has complied with the procedures, conditions, and prerequisites required for the original declaration, 1 year after the heir designation, the declarant may file an application in probate court to change the designation.

K. Penalty

Whenever a person is found guilty under the laws of this state or any ordinance of any political subdivision thereof, of operating a motor vehicle in violation of such laws or ordinances, relating to reckless operation, the trial court of any court of record may, in addition to or independent of all other penalties provided by law, suspend or revoke the driver's license or commercial driver's license of any person so convicted or pleading guilty to such offenses for such period as it determines, not to exceed one year.

The penalty for violating a state law or an ordinance of a political subdivision relating to reckless operation of a motor vehicle is the suspension or revocation of a driver's license or commercial driver's license for a time period fixed by the court, not to exceed one year. This penalty is in addition to other penalties provided by law.

L. Creation of an Entity or Office

There is hereby created an environmental board of review, consisting of three members appointed by the governor with the advice and consent of the Senate.

The environmental review board consists of three members appointed by the governor with the approval of the senate.

M. Cross References

[No example]

N. Numbers, Dates, Time, Age

1a. Cardinal numbers

A petition for reconsideration of an application must be filed with the department within ten days of notice of denial.

To seek reconsideration, an applicant shall file a petition with the department within 10 days of notice of denial.

1b. Ordinal numbers

Once a permit is twice denied, denial is final.

The second permit denial is final.

1c. Fractional numbers

Each board of elections shall exercise by a 2/3 vote all powers granted to such board by statute.

At least a two thirds vote is required for the board of elections to exercise a power granted by statute.

2. Dates

This Act shall become effective on the first of January 2005.

This act takes effect January 1, 2005

3a. Time of day

The department will be closed at half past three on each afternoon before a federal holiday.

The department shall close at 3:30 p.m. on the day before a federal holiday.

3b. Period of time

The luxury tax shall apply to such items that are purchased on or after the January 1, 2004.

The luxury tax applies to a purchase made after December 31, 2004.

4. Age

A "minor" means an individual who is 17 years of age or younger.

A "minor" means an individual under age 18.

O. Capital Letters

The State Board of Pharmacy shall establish controlled substance Schedules I, II, III, IV, and V.

The state board of pharmacy shall establish controlled substance schedules I, II, III, IV, and V.

P. Hyphens

Non-residents of the State may file with the Secretary of State for a license to use a trade name.

A nonresident of the state may file with the secretary of state for a license to use a trade name.

Index of Subjects and Words

References are to Pages

161

References are to Pages

†